the Jesus perspective

A Faith That May Surprise You

ROBERT HARRIS

509 PRESS

Durham, North Carolina

The Jesus Perspective:
A Faith that May Surprise You

©2019 Robert Harris

Published by 509 Press, Durham, North Carolina.
All rights reserved.

42/30/1.112319/p1.112919/p4.112920

A parable

Two men walked to a stream to retrieve water, and then headed back to their village.

The younger man, concerned, said, "Why do you have so much more water than I do? Why are you so blessed?"

The older man smiled and said, "Well, it might have something to do with the fact that I brought a bucket and you brought a cup."

Table of contents

The author

Robert Harris is a full-time writer and part-time theologian, inventor, and puzzle constructor. His books include *101 Things NOT to Do Before You Die*, *6 Keys to Writing Effectively*, *Sudden Forgiveness: Transforming Your Life in the Blink of an Eye,* and the *Claude Monet, Private Eye* mystery series.

Acknowledgement

I want to thank Liz Petersen for her careful reading and insightful comments during the preparation of this book.

Conventions

For convenience, I often will refer to the authors of biblical books in the conventional way—for example, Matthew as the author of the Gospel of Matthew. In fact, many books of the Bible were written by anonymous authors, or had multiple contributors.

Also, to avoid awkward sentences, I will refer to God in the traditional way as He, even though most would agree that God doesn't have a gender.

And finally, I will occasionally add *italics* to Scripture verses for emphasis. Unless otherwise noted, all Bible verses are from the New Revised Standard Version, accessed at https://www.christianity.com.

What this book is about

Five years ago I started examining the Christian faith—
my faith—with a critical eye. One goal was to discover
how the traditional beliefs originated, developed, and took
hold. Another goal was to determine which elements of
the faith were essential and useful, and which were not.

I had no idea what I was getting into! Each answer led
to many other questions. Each article I read led to a dozen
more. Each moment of enlightenment led to moments of
uncertainty. All in all, it's been a fascinating adventure. I
was often surprised, sometimes intrigued, and occasionally baffled. But at all times I was glad that I finally
undertook the project. And gradually I was able to acquire
a broad understanding of the key elements of my faith:
Bible, incarnation, atonement, trinity, and resurrection.

As I did my research, I tried to avoid the trap of merely
confirming my assumptions and preconceptions. I tried to
go where the facts led me. And I tried to assess diverse
opinions with an open mind. I was determined to find
authentic Christianity—the faith *of* Jesus, not the faith

about Jesus—free of the pointless theological complications that have been added over the centuries.

Along the way I had to discard ideas that I thought were carved in stone. I had to rethink what many would call the core beliefs of Christianity. And I had to critically assess principles that I always had taken for granted. It turns out that ignorance is not bliss—it's just comfortable and familiar. But I finally decided that it really wasn't a good foundation for my faith.

In this book, I want to share what I've learned and how it has reshaped my beliefs. I hope that my discoveries and insights will be helpful, and perhaps motivate others to do their own investigating so their faith also can become more useful, practical, and meaningful in everyday life. After all, questioning, scrutinizing, and learning are absolutely essential to a healthy and realistic faith life.

In the following chapters, I give an account of my effort to finally examine my faith and determine what is essential, what is relevant, and what is useful. It's been challenging work. But it's all been worth it because I now feel that I'm closer than ever to the remarkable faith of Jesus—the dynamic, vibrant, and empowering faith that I call *Path Christianity*. Keep reading to find out why!

1. Bible

Introduction

The Bible is a collection of books written by several dozen authors over a period of about 1500 years. It is considered sacred and used by Christians for inspiration and guidance. The Bible has been a perennial bestseller, and is available in its entirety in more than 650 languages.[1] It is perhaps the most influential collection of writings, having informed laws, cultural standards, and moral codes around the world for centuries. "Our intellectual heritage is full of its words and phrases, ideas and formulas."[2]

The Bible consists of two portions. The Old Testament, written mostly in Hebrew, records the experiences of the ancient Jewish people as they attempt to survive and thrive. The New Testament, written mostly in Greek, chronicles the experiences of the early Christians as they try to spread their new faith following the ministry of Jesus of Nazareth.

As a whole, the Bible is challenging to read and understand. It was produced long ago by people who saw the world and explained events in profoundly different ways than we do today. It uses imagery that we find bizarre, assumes norms that we no longer accept, and employs frameworks of thought that are foreign to us. Nevertheless it continues to be held in high esteem by much of the Christian community.

During the past century and a half, scholars have provided an increasingly clear, detailed, and fascinating understanding of the books of the Bible: who wrote them, why they wrote them, to whom they wrote them, and when they wrote them. Some people object that scholarship has "attacked" the authority of Scripture; others have welcomed the objective approach that teases apart the historical and theological aspects.

Conventional view

The conventional Christian view is that the Bible is the inerrant, infallible word of God. It was written by men who were directly inspired by God, and speaks with one authoritative voice. All parts of it are true and useful, and all parts contribute to a unified message.

I began researching these claims so I could gain a more complete understanding of them. I wanted to see if I could determine whether they all were accurate, useful, and essential to my Christian faith.

In this chapter, I'll talk about some of the questions I've asked and the answers and speculations I've found. I'll try to explain how they have helped to shape my understanding of the Bible.

Is the Bible the inspired word of God?

All of my life I've heard that the Bible is divinely inspired, or "God-breathed." And I thought that this was one of the distinguishing features of my faith. But it turns out that the idea of special inspiration is not unique to the Judeo-Christian tradition. All religions have documents that are considered sacred, holy, and divinely inspired.

For example, followers of Islam revere the Quran, which is believed to have been revealed to Muhammad over a period of two decades. And in Hinduism, the "heard" teachings, or sruti, are "considered divinely inspired and fully authoritative for belief and practice..."[3]

But in the Christian world, it is the Bible that is considered inspired. Why? People typically point to one verse penned in the mid first century by Paul of Tarsus, an early advocate for the Christian faith:

> All scripture is inspired by God and is useful for teaching, for reproof, for correction, and for training in righteousness.[4]

I learned about logical fallacies way back in the ninth grade,[5] so I recognize a circular argument when I see one: Scripture is inspired because Scripture says so!

But just because the logic is suspect doesn't necessarily mean that the conclusion is wrong. So I wanted to see if it made sense. I wanted to see if I could determine whether the Bible's writers were at all times inspired by God.

I first considered these two verses:

> You shall not round off the hair on your temples or mar the edges of your beard.[6]

> "Whatever you ask for in prayer with faith, you will receive."[7]

I realized that there was no way to know without doubt if the writers of these two verses were divinely inspired.

But I *could* decide, without any difficulty, if what they wrote is *inspiring*. The obvious answer was *no* to the first verse and *yes* to the second.

It soon became clear that I could, using my heart and mind, easily distinguish the inspiring from the uninspiring passages. So I wondered if I should be more concerned with the inspirational quality of ideas and less with where and how they originated. Then I would have a practical way to evaluate what I find in the Bible.

With this new perspective in mind, I looked at a few more verses to see what I could conclude about them:

> The sons of Eliphaz were Teman, Omar, Zepho, Gatam, and Kenaz. (Timna was a concubine of Eliphaz, Esau's son; she bore Amalek to Eliphaz.) These were the sons of Adah, Esau's wife.[8] *Informative, but not inspiring.*

> That very night the angel of the Lord set out and struck down one hundred eighty-five thousand in the camp of the Assyrians; when morning dawned, they were all dead bodies.[9] *Frightening, but not inspiring.*

> Like a gold ring in a pig's snout is a beautiful woman without good sense.[10] *Amusing (and vivid), but not inspiring.*

Then I looked at a few more verses that had a noticeably different quality:

> The Lord is my shepherd, I shall not want.[11] *Inspiring.*

> ...those who wait for the Lord shall renew their strength, they shall mount up with wings like eagles, they shall run and not be weary, they shall walk and not faint.[12] *Inspiring.*

> "You are the light of the world...let your light
> shine before others, so that they may see your
> good works and give glory to your Father in
> heaven."[13] *Inspiring.*

Throughout the Bible I was able to find many ideas, guidelines, and accounts that were inspiring—but also many that were not. So I realized that I no longer had to try to force every element of the Bible into the "divinely inspired" category. It wasn't necessary or useful. After all, as theologian Marcus Borg asserts, the Bible "...is not God's witness to God (not a Divine product) but [the ancient Jewish and early Christian communities'] witness to God."[14]

Many believe that the Bible *must* be seen as wholly inspired or else "...the gospel, the church, and Christianity itself are all just smoke-and-mirrors."[15] This, I think, is melodramatic and not at all a realistic or useful point of view.

What did Jesus think?

According to the Gospel accounts, Jesus never commented about Scripture (the Hebrew Bible, or what we know as the Old Testament) being wholly inspired. He did hold it in high regard, however, and quoted frequently from it. So he obviously thought that particular ideas presented in it were inspiring and of value to his listeners. But he certainly believed that some ideas were *not* inspiring and *not* of value, judging from the fact that he expressed his dissatisfaction with them.

For example, the Old Testament view concerning oaths was this:

> The Lord your God you shall fear; him you shall
> serve, and by his name alone you shall swear.[16]

But Jesus must have thought swearing by God's name to be uninspiring, because he taught this:

> "Let your word be 'Yes, Yes' or 'No, No'; anything more than this comes from the evil one."[17]

And the Old Testament view about the Sabbath was this:

> ...the seventh day is a sabbath to the Lord your God; you shall not do any work...[18]

But Jesus surely found that uninspiring because he routinely went about teaching and healing on the Sabbath. Here's what he had to say about the matter:

> ..."Suppose one of you has only one sheep and it falls into a pit on the sabbath; will you not lay hold of it and lift it out? How much more valuable is a human being than a sheep! So it is lawful to do good on the sabbath."[19]

Again and again, Jesus showed that he was not concerned with the *origins* of ideas and principles, only with their practical value. However, he did say this:

> ..."Blessed rather are those who hear the word of God and obey it!"[20]

But he didn't teach that the *written law* (the Hebrew Bible) perfectly and completely captured the "word of God." He used a commonsense approach and evaluated scriptural messages in terms of their ability to inspire individuals to grow spiritually and seek God's kingdom.

Conclusion

The idea that the Bible is wholly inspired doesn't hold up to even modest scrutiny. A great deal of what it contains is uninspiring, unhelpful, or confusing. Furthermore, some of it condones violence, some promotes misguided values and mores, and some encourages the devaluation of certain groups and individuals. Thus much of the Bible couldn't have come directly from God.

But the Bible *does* contain a great many ideas, guidelines, and accounts that are *inspiring*. I just have to use my full capacity for understanding—my reason and my intuition—to identify them. Instead of asking whether a passage of Scripture is inspired (and always answering *yes*), I will from now on ask a more pertinent question: Does it inspire me to live more abundantly?

Jesus clearly saw much in the Bible of his day that he thought was inspiring. But he didn't talk about divine inspiration of every word of Scripture and insist that people accept that notion. And it seems like something he would have stressed over and over if it had been essential. He focused not on the *source* of inspiring ideas, but on their potential *impact* on human lives.

Is the Bible completely inerrant?

Another widely held belief about the Bible is that it is free of errors and contradictions. The idea has been around for quite a while, and ties in with the notion of divine inspiration. The philosopher Augustine of Hippo, in the fourth century, thought it to be essential to the faith:

> "It seems to me that the most disastrous consequences must follow upon our believing that anything false is found in the sacred books: that is to say that the men by whom the Scripture has been given to us, and committed to writing, did put down in these books anything false..."[21]

And the *Westminster Confession of Faith*, written in England in 1646, states it this way:

> "The authority of the Holy Scripture, for which it
> ought to be believed, and obeyed, dependeth not
> upon the testimony of any man, or church; but
> wholly upon God (who is truth itself) the author
> thereof: and therefore it is to be received, be-
> cause it is the Word of God."[22]

These are very strong, confident, and unambiguous statements. But with all due respect to Augustine and the Westminster folks, I was able to find a great many errors in the Bible without difficulty. But they were not all of one type.

Lots of the errors seem inconsequential. For example, the people of Israel were predicted to be enslaved in Egypt for 400 years,[23] and it turned out to be 430 years.[24]

Other errors obviously weren't seen as errors originally, but were *revealed* as our understanding of the cosmos, and our grasp of natural laws, advanced over time. For example, we no longer attribute diseases to the actions of malicious, invisible demons.

Other errors exist because assumptions made by the writers are no longer valid. For example, the assumption that slavery is acceptable, and the assumption that women have less value than men.

And other errors are present in the Bible because of faulty copying and translation. For example, Jesus most likely referred to a hawser (ship's rope) going through the eye of a needle, not a camel.[25] As theologian William Barclay points out, "the Greek word for camel is *kamēlos;* the Greek word for ship's hawser is *kamīlos.*"[26]

Finally, some errors exist because the Bible presents conflicting versions of events. For example, in Genesis we learn that humans were created *after* the animals,[27] and also that humans were created *before* the animals.[28]

Even the early church fathers recognized that Scripture contained inconsistencies and errors. And they solved the problem using allegory. Whenever a passage presented an idea that seemed untrue or at odds with another passage, it was simply interpreted in terms of its "deeper meaning." In other words, inerrancy was *forced* on the Bible by imaginative interpretations of words and phrases.

But, as many have pointed out, it is a flawed method. Thomas Aquinas, in the thirteenth century, recognized the dangers of relying on allegory:

> "For many different senses in one text produce confusion and deception and destroy all force of argument. Hence no argument, but only fallacies, can be deduced from a multiplicity of propositions."[29]

Fortunately, allegory is largely a thing of the past (however, it is still popular with some, as we shall see later). But in its place is *harmonization*, the valiant effort to make everything in the Bible fit perfectly with everything else. No matter what kind of errors are found, the harmonizers convert them to "apparent errors" by changing the meanings of words to support their contention of inerrancy.

During my research, I've come across some of the most ludicrous reasoning and tortured logic employed by people who are determined to make all inconsistencies and errors disappear. But I now see it as a pointless effort. The Bible presents ideas in various stages of development. Mature thought, arrived at after centuries of experience, can't realistically be harmonized with primitive thought. And conflicting accounts can't, with intellectual honesty, be reconciled simply by changing the meanings of selected words.

What did Jesus think?

Jesus often used Scripture to make a point or bolster an argument. But as far as I can tell, he didn't explicitly say anything about Scripture being completely free of errors. In fact, it's clear that he thought the writers had erred in a number of instances because he frequently offered alternative views.

For example, regarding divorce, the Old Testament position was this:

> Suppose a man enters into marriage with a
> woman, but she does not please him because he
> finds something objectionable about her, and so
> he writes her a certificate of divorce, puts it in
> her hand, and sends her out of his house; she
> then leaves his house.[30]

But Jesus evidently recognized that this convention was unfair to women and therefore erroneous. He said:

> "...So they are no longer two, but one flesh.
> Therefore what God has joined together, let no
> one separate."[31]

And regarding revenge, the Old Testament position was this:

> If any harm follows, then you shall give life for
> life, eye for eye, tooth for tooth, hand for hand...[32]

But Jesus must have thought this concept to be immature and therefore erroneous. He said:

> "You have heard that it was said, 'An eye for an
> eye and a tooth for a tooth.' But I say to you, Do
> not resist an evildoer. But if anyone strikes you
> on the right cheek, turn the other also."[33]

There are many other examples, but these two illustrate that Jesus acknowledged errors in the Bible of his day and didn't hesitate to offer his own way of looking at things. He readily corrected what he thought was erroneous so people would have more reliable and useful guidance for living righteously.

Conclusion

The idea that the Bible is wholly inerrant can't be reconciled with what the text actually says. There are a great many errors and inconsistencies, some of which are minor and some of which are more significant. The attempt to make the errors go away through imaginative interpretation is misguided. The harmonization process manipulates what the Bible's writers actually said about God, immortality, right and wrong, and other fundamental concerns.

But the Bible *does* contain many ideas, guidelines, and accounts that, over time, have come to be seen as inerrant. They have been worked out in people's lives for more than a hundred generations in every conceivable type of situation. Today I can, without difficulty, find many passages that undeniably convey truth that is relevant to my development and spiritual growth.

Jesus identified in the Bible of his day certain ideas that were erroneous. Some he recognized as unfair; others as being out of date; others as being nonessential; and others as being immature or incomplete. He didn't insist that people accept the idea that all Scripture was inerrant. But he obviously believed that some ideas in it were, without doubt, inerrant. He focused on those principles that, when fully grasped and sincerely tried, reliably brought about positive change in individuals.

Is the Bible wholly infallible?

Biblical infallibility refers to the widespread belief that the Bible is completely trustworthy as a guide to matters of faith and salvation. The idea has been one of the dominant themes of Christianity since the Bible as we know it came together.

John Wesley, the founder of Methodism, said that the Bible was

> "...the great means God has ordained for conveying his manifold grace to man," and that "all Scripture is infallibly true..."[34]

And some, like theologian Norman Geisler, insist that infallibility is absolutely essential to the Christian faith:

> "Every Christian doctrine—whether it's about God, sin or salvation—is drawn from the Bible. If we can't trust the Bible, then we've lost the very foundation of our faith."[35]

I wondered if this all-or-none position was reasonable. After all, the 66 books of the Bible must have a great deal to say about faith and salvation. But the writings come from a variety of places and cultures over a period of more than 1500 years. Could it all of it be equally trustworthy and reliable in today's world?

Although the concepts of faith and salvation have many dimensions, I focused on two obvious ones: how we see God, and how we interact with God. I wanted to see if the Bible presents wholly trustworthy and reliable information concerning these dimensions.

How we see God

I first wanted to look for information about the object of faith: God. As you might expect, I found that the Bible writers had a lot to say about God. Here are some things I learned:

> God was initially imagined to be a storm god who lived on a mountain; later we find that "God is spirit" and not bound to a place.[36]

> God was seen as a tribal war god; later we find that "God is love."[37]

> God was seen as one of many tribal deities; later we find that He is the one universal Father.

> God inspired fear and dread; later He was seen as an indwelling spirit who is our constant friend.[38]

God might not change over time, but the way the Bible's writers imagined Him changed substantially. So it would be wrong to say that all of the various ideas about God in our modern Bibles are equally trustworthy.

How we interact with God

I then looked for information about how we can and should interact with God (to please Him generally and to seek reconciliation).

Early on, following Jewish law to the letter was a large part of trying to do God's will and gain His favor. In the Torah, there are no fewer than 613 criminal, ceremonial, and moral laws that were intended to keep everyone on the right track so God would be inclined to be helpful and merciful.[39]

Concerning reconciliation, the focus in the ancient Jewish world was on performing sacrifices. In Leviticus, five types of sacrifices are described that were intended to restore a torn relationship with God: the burnt offering (for general atonement of sin), the grain offering (an

expression of devotion to God), the peace offering (to en-
sure peace and prosperity), the sin offering (for the atonement of unintentional sin), and the guilt offering (to make
reparations for one's sins).[40]

But much later we find other ideas about reconciliation
recorded in the Bible:

> For by grace you have been saved through faith,
> and this is not your own doing; it is the gift of
> God.[41]

> You see that a person is justified by works and
> not by faith alone.[42]

> They answered, "Believe on the Lord Jesus, and
> you will be saved, you and your household."

So there are a number of different views in Scripture
about how to interact with God and what to expect for our
efforts. They can't all be equally trustworthy and reliable.
But they are all present in the Bibles that we use today.

What did Jesus think?

Jesus valued Scripture, and obviously saw in it some
information that he felt was infallible. In fact, when trying
to support an idea, he frequently used the phrase "it is
written" when referring to scriptural passages that he
thought to be significant. But he never asserted that the
Bible was *wholly* trustworthy in matters of faith and salvation.

The ancient Jewish people had very precise ways of
pleasing God and interacting with Him. It was a straightforward and easy-to-grasp system. Jesus, on the other
hand, didn't frame faith and salvation in terms of performing ritualistic sacrifices or following long lists of rules.
Instead, he talked about them using vivid imagery and
relatively vague language.

About God he said:

> "...If a shepherd has a hundred sheep, and one of them has gone astray, does he not leave the ninety-nine on the mountains and go in search of the one that went astray? And if he finds it, truly I tell you, he rejoices over it more than over the ninety-nine that never went astray."[43]

And about faith he said:

> "...For truly I tell you, if you have faith the size of a mustard seed, you will say to this mountain, 'Move from here to there,' and it will move; and nothing will be impossible for you."[44]

> "Ask, and it will be given you; search, and you will find; knock, and the door will be opened for you."[45]

And about reconciliation Jesus said:

> "Not everyone who says to me, 'Lord, Lord,' will enter the kingdom of heaven, but only the one who does the will of my Father in heaven."[46]

> ..."Repent, for the kingdom of heaven has come near."[47]

> "Truly I tell you, whoever does not receive the kingdom of God as a little child will never enter it."[48]

These were not straightforward do's and don'ts. Nor did Jesus oversimplify faith and salvation to make them easy to understand. He challenged his listeners to grapple with these profound matters and try to grasp their essence.

Conclusion

The Bible is not wholly infallible in matters of faith and salvation because it presents a variety of ideas that can't be reconciled. Many ideas are not trustworthy guides because they are immature, incomplete, or outdated. Yet they remain in the Bible. So trying to force the "infallible" label on everything I find in Scripture seems futile. And it limits the value of critical thinking, which is never a good idea.

But the Bible *does* contain many profound and infallible guidelines that can help me to grow spiritually. In its pages are ideas that are timeless and unchangeable. Consider this: "Blessed are the pure in heart, for they will see God."[49] It's hard to imagine anything that would ever make that assertion less reliable.

Jesus didn't teach that the Bible was wholly infallible in matters of faith and salvation. But he did focus on both old and new ideas that *were* infallible in the sense that *they worked when properly understood and applied.* Jesus focused on timeless principles that could, without doubt, help people comprehend the essentials of faith and salvation, and live more abundantly.

Does the Bible present a unified message?

Many Christians insist that the Bible speaks with a single voice and presents a coherent and unified story, even though at least forty writers contributed its more than 750,000 words.

Some simply make sweeping claims. For example, evangelical author A. W. Pink says that in the output of the Bible's authors, we find that there is "...perfect accord and concord, unison and unity, harmony in all their teachings, and the same conceptions pervading all their writings..."[50]

But does merely proclaiming the Bible's unity make it unified?

Others say that unity is demonstrated by the mere fact that some ideas are mentioned at different times and by different individuals. For example, the fact that the great flood was noted by Moses, the apostle Peter, and Jesus is sometimes given as proof.[51] But does demonstrating knowledge of a past event actually mean that writers were adding chapters to an existing story?

Others have used a more creative approach to impose unity on the Bible. For example, evangelist Billy Graham finds Jesus in each of the Old Testament books:

> "The story of Jesus can be traced through the
> Bible. In Genesis, He is the Seed of the Woman. In
> Exodus, He is the Passover Lamb. In Leviticus,
> He is the Atoning Sacrifice. In Numbers, He is the
> Smitten Rock...In Esther, He is the Advocate. In
> Job, He is My Redeemer. In Psalms, He is My
> Song..."[52]

Using this allegorical approach, a lamb is not a lamb and a rock is not a rock—they are whatever they need to be to create the desired unified story.

I'm sure that people who engage in this sort of activity have good intentions—but they are using a bad and unreliable method. Allegorizing would be useful only if each person's imaginative interpretations coincided with those of everyone else.

Many have (wisely) abandoned allegorical interpretation. Today, people are more likely to use the harmonization process to force the Bible's many disparate elements into a single coherent story written by a single author.

But harmonization is not just something employed by commentators to deal with, say, the two different genealogies of Jesus presented in Matthew and Luke, or the two different versions of the Ten Commandments found in Exodus. It is actually built into most Bible translations.

For example, the popular New International Version (NIV) is replete with mistranslations that are used to do away with obvious inconsistencies and errors.

Consider this account in 2 Chronicles (in the NIV):

> Ahaziah was twenty-two years old when he became king...[53]

According to biblical researcher Paul Davidson:

> "All Hebrew manuscripts give Ahaziah's age as 'forty-two,' but the NIV changes it to 'twenty-two' to harmonize the text with 2 Kings 8:26."[54]

Davidson also cites several dozen other deliberate mistranslations intended to make the Bible speak with one consistent voice. Some of the changes are minor; but some, as I will emphasize later in this book, are significant and have had a profound impact on Christian beliefs.

So harmonization is used to create in the Bible a coherent story with a single author. But this result is achieved only if we bend and shape selected words and accounts to mean what we *would like* them to mean rather than what they *actually* mean. And if we do that, we miss the real story: that people who diligently seek God can grow spiritually. They gradually can overcome immature ideas and follow more enlightened paths that are in alignment with divine purpose.

What did Jesus think?

Jesus was familiar with the Bible of his day, and most certainly knew that it contained different and incompatible ideas, guidelines, and accounts. From what I was able to gather, he didn't try to harmonize it all and insist that everyone find one unified story in Scripture. Nor did he put himself in each Old Testament story to create unity. In fact, he never said that the Hebrew Bible presented a single message.

However, Jesus' teachings do create a certain continuity with what came before. He routinely referred to inherited ideas: "until the law is fulfilled"; "it is written"; "you have heard that it was said."

And he enthusiastically brought forward the teaching of the Old Testament to love God "with all your heart, and with all your soul, and with all your might."[55] To it he added this:

"You shall love your neighbor as yourself."[56]

And in the New Testament writings of Paul and others, we see an emphasis on selected ideas from the Hebrew Bible and from Jesus' teachings. But continuity is not the same as unity. It merely shows that some ideas have true value that isn't affected by time and change.

Conclusion

The Bible clearly does not speak with just one voice and present just one basic message. In its pages I can find a variety of messages about God, immortality, salvation, and many other significant topics. Certain themes are carried through the Bible—but that doesn't imply a single author. I can't make the Bible wholly consistent and unified without performing mental gymnastics to make all of the elements conform to a well-organized story.

But the Bible does, in many cases, speak with a most *convincing* voice—one that transcends time and change. I need to use my heart and mind to recognize the ideas, guidelines, and accounts that convey truths about universal human concerns. I need to look not for a single *story*, but for a single *desire*—to know God—that is manifested in a wide variety of ways.

Jesus didn't seem concerned with making all of his teachings fit perfectly with what was recorded in the Old Testament. (And we now know that his teachings don't mesh perfectly with New Testament thought, either.) When Jesus offered guidance, he readily used inherited ideas—but only those that could help people to understand their true value, grow spiritually, and live more abundantly.

Summary

Five years ago, I was seriously uninformed about the Bible, and believed that the conventional view of it was the only reasonable and accepted one. But after a good deal of research, I gradually was able to leave my ignorance behind. I attempted to replace it with an understanding rooted in facts, common sense, and rational interpretations, and less restricted by preconceptions.

Update to what I know

I no longer see the Bible as a static collection of timeless truths handed down from above, but a dynamic human record of the development of key ideas over time.

The Bible is clearly not wholly inspired (and inspiring), wholly inerrant, wholly infallible, or wholly useful. But to me, that doesn't diminish its value. It just means that I have to use the Bible differently than I once did. Instead of docilely accepting everything that I find in it as coming from God, I need to examine what I read. My approach to the Bible is now practical. Whenever I read anything in it, I ask:

• Does it motivate me to grow spiritually?

• Does it inspire me to live abundantly?

• Does it encourage me to let my light shine and thus glorify God?

I think that the Bible contains useful guidance and many inspiring accounts, inerrant ideas, and infallible principles. I just need to find them among the less significant parts. To me, something either has value or it does not. And the way I can decide is by evaluating it using my heart and mind, and by trying it out in my life.

So I no longer see the Bible as "God's word" except in the sense that it contains elements that I believe are in alignment with divine purpose. And I think that it is worthwhile to try to discover what those elements are.

Course change

Considering what I've learned during the past few years, I have decided to part with the conventional church view of the Bible and instead to follow Jesus. Although he respected the Bible of his time, he obviously didn't accept everything in it as being inspired, true, and useful. He distinguished the essential ideas from the nonessential, and separated the out-of-date principles from the timeless ones.

Jesus saw the Bible as a document that must be interpreted carefully with both heart and mind. And he understood the need to use a *flexible* approach so that people and their needs always came ahead of biblical laws, rituals, and ceremonies. He rejected ideas in the Bible that seemed immature, unfair, incomplete, or inconsequential. But he embraced ideas in it that seemed helpful, inspiring, and profound. I think his approach makes sense. And I think I can benefit more from following it than from adhering to a church doctrine.

So the traditional view—that the Bible is wholly inerrant, infallible, and inspired—is no longer tenable. My

Christian faith no longer depends on the Bible being a particular type of *document*. It depends on Jesus being a particular type of *individual:* someone who understood that Scripture needs to be continually evaluated to identify its flaws, inadequacies, and errors, and to discover its transformative ideas. Thus the Bible is no longer a static collection of truths. Instead, it is a collection of diverse ideas, and interpreting them involves a dynamic process in which I can *participate*. What a positive and practical perspective!

Notes

[1] "Why Bible Translation?" Wycliffe, 2019, https://www.wycliffe.org/about/why
[2] Fosdick, Harry Emerson. The *Modern Use of the Bible*. New York: The Macmillan Company, 1924, page 3.
[3] "Hindu Sacred Texts." ReligionFacts, 2016, http://www.religionfacts.com/hinduism/texts
[4] 2 Timothy 3:16
[5] Chase, Stuart. *Guides to Straight Thinking*. New York: Harper, 1956.
[6] Leviticus 19:27
[7] Matthew 21:22
[8] Genesis 36:11-12
[9] 2 Kings 19:35
[10] Proverbs 11:22
[11] Psalm 23
[12] Isaiah 40:31
[13] Mark 5:14, 16
[14] Borg, Marcus. *The Heart of Christianity: Rediscovering a Life of Faith*. San Francisco: HarperOne, 2009.

[15] Menikoff, Aaron. "Is the Bible Reliable for Truth about Jesus Christ?" The Gospel Coalition, 2009, https://www.thegospelcoalition.org/article/is-the-bible-reliable-for-truth-about-jesus-christ/

[16] Deuteronomy 6:13

[17] Matthew 5:37

[18] Deuteronomy 5:14

[19] Matthew 12:11-12

[20] Luke 11:28

[21] Woodbridge, John. "Did Fundamentalists Invent Inerrancy?" The Gospel Coalition, 2017, https://www.thegospelcoalition.org/article/did-fundamentalists-invent-inerrancy/

[22] *The Confession of Faith*. Presbyterian Church in America, 2012, https://www.pcaac.org/wp-content/uploads/2012/11/WCFScriptureProofs.pdf

[23] Genesis 15:13

[24] Exodus 12:40-41

[25] Matthew 19:24

[26] Barclay, William, cited in Lorah, Jr., Theodore R. "Again—Camel or Rope in Matthew 19.24 and Mark 10.25?" Palmer Seminary, 1996, http://tmcdaniel.palmerseminary.edu/camel-hawser.pdf

[27] Genesis 1:25-27

[28] Genesis 2:18-19

[29] Aquinas, Thomas. *Summa Theologiae*. Benzinger Brothers Printers to the Holy Apostolic See, 1485, http://www.newadvent.org/summa/1001.htm

[30] Deuteronomy 24:1

[31] Mark 10:8-9

[32] Exodus 21:23-24

[33] Matthew 5:38-39

[34] "The Sermons of John Wesley - Sermon 16: The Means of Grace." Wesley Center Online, http://wesley.nnu.edu/john-wesley/the-sermons-of-john-wesley-1872-edition/sermon-16-the-means-of-grace/

[35] Geisler, Norman. "Take a Stand on Biblical Inerrancy." Billy Graham Evangelistic Association, 2014, https://billygraham.org/decision-magazine/may-2014/take-a-stand-on-biblical-inerrancy/

[36] John 4:24

[37] 1 John 4:16

[38] Fosdick, Harry Emerson. *A Guide to Understanding the Bible*. New York: Harper & Row, 1938.

[39] Kohler, Kauffmann and Broydé, Isaac. "Commandments, The 613." Jewish Encyclopedia, 1906, http://www.jewishencyclopedia.com/articles/4566-commandments-the-613

[40] Garrett, Jeremiah K. "The 5 Offerings in the Old Testament." *Seedbed*, Asbury Theological Seminary, 2014, https://www.seedbed.com/5-offerings-old-testament/

[41] Ephesians 2:8

[42] James 2:24

[43] Matthew 18:12-13

[44] Matthew 17:20

[45] Matthew 7:7

[46] Matthew 7:21

[47] Matthew 4:17

[48] Luke 18:17

[49] Matthew 5:8

[50] Pink, A. W. "The Wonderful Unity of the Bible Attests Its Divine Authorship." *Monergism*, CPR Foundation, 2018, https://www.monergism.com/wonderful-unity-bible-attests-its-divine-authorship-w-pink

[51] Chaffey, Tim. "Unity of the Bible: Seven Compelling Evidences." Answers in Genesis, 2014, https://answersingenesis.org/the-word-of-god/3-unity-of-the-bible/

[52] Graham, Billy. "The Bible: The Word of God." *Decision Magazine*, Billy Graham Evangelistic Association, 2019, https://billygraham.org/decision-magazine/march-2019/bible-word-of-god/

[53] 2 Chronicles 22:2 (NIV)

[54] Davidson, Paul. "Poor and Misleading Translation in the New International Version (NIV)," https://isthatinthebible.wordpress.com/articles-and-resources/deliberate-mistranslation-in-the-new-international-version-niv/

[55] Deuteronomy 6:5

[56] Matthew 22:39

2. Incarnation

Introduction

The word "incarnation" means "the embodiment of a deity or spirit in some earthly form,"[1] and derives from the Latin *in+carnis*, meaning "in the flesh."[2] But *"the* Incarnation" is generally understood to mean the traditional Christian interpretation of the concept:

> "...God assumed a human nature and became a man in the form of Jesus Christ, the Son of God and the second person of the Trinity."[3]

Incarnation is not a universal theme in religions. Judaism and Islam, for example, do not accept the idea of God becoming incarnate. But in Hinduism, avatars are seen as bodily incarnations of deities, appearing on earth to restore *dharma*, the path of righteousness. However, an avatar typically will be killed or go back to its previous existence. In Christianity, Jesus is considered to be "God with us" not just for a while, but for all time.[4]

Belief in incarnation implies the belief that God is close, not distant; that He is concerned, not indifferent; that He is active, not passive, in human affairs. But even if we accept the concept of incarnation, we naturally speculate about how, when, and where it came about—or *comes* about. And the history of Christianity is a history of debates about incarnation, among other weighty matters.

Conventional view

The conventional Christian view of incarnation is that the Bible teaches that God the Son entered the world in the man Jesus of Nazareth. He fulfilled prophecy by being born of a virgin, thereby avoiding a sinful nature. He was at the same time both fully God and fully human, representing a unique union of human and divine natures.

I began looking into these ideas to become better informed about them. How did they originate and develop? Are they reasonable and warranted? Do they help me in any practical way? And are they vital to my Christian faith?

In this chapter, I'll present an overview of what I've learned about incarnation, and explain how and why my view of it has changed.

Is the concept of incarnation found in the Bible?

According to the *HarperCollins Bible Dictionary*, the term "incarnation"

> "...does not appear in the [New Testament], but the elements of the doctrine are present in different stages of development."[5]

If we want to go looking for those elements, the best place to start seems to be the New Testament documents that were written the soonest after Jesus' death, and also the Gospels.

Earliest New Testament books

Many scholars believe that James is the earliest book that now appears in the New Testament, having been written only a dozen years or so after Jesus. In it, there is no mention of Jesus as being God who came into the world by supernatural means.

The second oldest document, written soon after James, is probably Paul's letter to the Christians in Galatia. In it he gives the first known account of Jesus' birth:

> But when the fullness of time had come, God sent
> his Son, *born of a woman, born under the law...*[6]

Here Paul doesn't identify Jesus as being specially born as God incarnate, only as one sent by God and born in a conventional way.

A few years later, in his letter to the Christians in Philippi, Paul writes this:

> *Let the same mind be in you that was in Christ
> Jesus*, who, though he was in the form of God, did
> not regard equality with God as something to be
> exploited...[7]

Here, Paul seems to be saying that Jesus was not a person apart from all others. Paul's opinion is that we all can have the "same mind" (understanding) that Jesus had and, like him, can become aware of our "innate Oneness with the divinity of God."[8]

The Gospel of Mark

Mark, the first Gospel written (circa 70), and therefore the one closest in time to the events being chronicled, says nothing at all about Jesus' birth. If stories about Jesus being God incarnate were circulating in the mid first century, it's hard to imagine that Mark would have failed to incorporate them into his account.

The Gospel of Matthew

Matthew, written about 15 years after Mark, is the first Gospel to suggest that Jesus' birth was special—so special, in fact, that his conception was accomplished by God's spirit. But the actual birth is described in ordinary terms, except that it was accompanied by a special star that guided wise men to Bethlehem so they could visit Jesus.

In this account, Matthew identifies Jesus as savior and messiah, but does not say that he was God who came to earth for the first and only time.

The Gospel of Luke

Luke (circa 85–95) provides the only other birth story. It is the more familiar one, and parallels Matthew's account in some ways: Jesus is conceived by holy spirit and is born in Bethlehem. But it differs in a few details. In this account, Jesus is born in a manger, his birth is announced by a "heavenly host," and the first people to visit Jesus are shepherds.

Like Matthew, Luke refers to Jesus as savior and messiah, but does not express the opinion that he was God in human form.

The Gospel of John

In John, written sixty years or more after Jesus, we don't find a story of Jesus' birth. But we do find this intriguing speculation about the nature of Jesus:

> In the beginning was the Word, and the Word
> was with God, and the Word was God...And the
> Word became flesh and lived among us...[9]

In the opening of his Gospel, John takes the Greek idea of *logos* ("the controlling principle of the universe") and applies it in his theology as "the eternal thought or word of God, made incarnate in Jesus Christ."[10]

Although translators have rendered "logos" as "word," it is a complex concept that has been interpreted in many ways. John seems to be adopting the meaning advanced by Philo, a Hellenistic Jewish philosopher. He transformed *logos*

> "from an abstract, impersonal force into a
> person with a mind and a will. Philo's Logos...
> was primarily an intermediary being who was
> needed to bridge the enormous gap between
> God...and the material world..."[11]

John, by incorporating the *logos* idea, tries to make Christianity more appealing to people in the Hellenistic world who were not familiar with Jewish concepts—messiahship, for example.

In summary, in New Testament writings we learn that someone special—savior, messiah, *logos*—arrived in the person Jesus. But the special one is never identified as God incarnate. Jesus is sometimes called "son of God," but he is never identified as the unique God-man.

What did Jesus think?

As far as we know, Jesus never talked about incarnation. He didn't tell anyone that he was the long awaited Emmanuel. Jesus was familiar with Scripture and quoted from it frequently. So he surely was aware of predictions about a coming messiah. But he never referenced them.

Jesus didn't claim that God entered earthly life through him, creating a unique person with two natures. If he had thought that such a notion would benefit people in their spiritual development, he certainly would have told them about it.

But Jesus evidently did recognize that God is within us, that He enters human affairs not just in one person, but in all persons. Consider what he said:

> "... if you have faith the size of a mustard seed, you will say to this mountain, 'Move from here to there,' and it will move..."[12]

If God is not within us—incarnate in us—whence this power?

And Jesus also said this:

> "You are the light of the world..."[13]

If God is not within us—incarnate in us—whence this status?

Conclusion

The traditional view of incarnation—that one of the three God-persons of a holy trinity entered human existence in the man Jesus—is not explicitly put forth in the Bible. Paul doesn't say that Jesus was the one and only God incarnate. He does state his opinion that God sent Jesus for a special purpose. But he doesn't identify Jesus as the unique God-man. If the idea of Jesus' being God incarnate had been known at the time, Paul surely would have mentioned it because of its motivational value.

In the Gospels, there are references to a miraculous birth in Matthew and Luke. But it was the birth of a *man*. Jesus was presented as savior and messiah, not as God incarnate. And although John imagines Jesus to be preexistent, he doesn't identify Jesus as God who came to earth in human form.

Jesus never said anything about being the one and only incarnation of God. He didn't say anything suggesting that he thought himself to be the *logos*, the divine reason in the cosmos, made flesh. He did allow people to call him "son of God," but that doesn't imply that he saw himself as God.

Was Jesus born of a virgin?

The idea that Jesus was virgin born has been important to many Christians for centuries, and is mentioned in creeds, hymns, and faith statements. And I always thought that the virgin birth was one of the distinctive features of the Christian faith. But I found out that accounts of virgin births have appeared in a variety of cultures.

> "Miraculous births, whether virgin or otherwise,
> are commonplace motifs in ancient literature
> and culture since such an event clearly signposts
> a very important being coming into the world."[14]

In the Christian faith, the virgin birth has captured the imagination of believers for many generations. And to find the origin of the idea, we need to go all the way back to the late first century—about fifty years *after* Jesus.

The Gospel of Matthew

In writing the first chapters of Matthew, the author does a fascinating thing. He takes a vague 800-year old prediction by Isaiah—that *someone, someday, somewhere* would be called Emmanuel ("God is with us")—and connects it to Jesus.

> "Eager to convince Jews that Jesus was God's
> promised messiah, Matthew planted references
> to the Hebrew Scriptures throughout his Gospel
> like clues in a mystery novel."[15]

In the best known example, Matthew describes an appearance of an angel to Joseph, who tells him that Mary will bear a son who "will save his people from their sins."[16] Matthew then says that the encounter took place

> ...to fulfill what had been spoken by the Lord
> through the prophet: "Look, the virgin shall
> conceive and bear a son, and they shall name

him Emmanuel," which means, "God is with us."[17]

The prophet he quotes, of course, is Isaiah. It was Isaiah's prediction that inspired Matthew. But I discovered that there's a problem here involving the Hebrew word *almah*, found in the original version of Isaiah. The word

> "...has traditionally been translated as 'virgin,' but research reveals that more likely it means 'a young woman of marriageable age' (*that is*, old enough to bear a child) without any specific indication of whether or not she is a virgin. This is reflected in most modern translations."[18]

Matthew's Bible was the Septuagint, the Greek translation of the Hebrew Bible created 300 years earlier. In it, the word for "young woman"(*almah*) was translated as "virgin" (even though Hebrew has a word for "virgin": *bethulah*). Matthew decides that Isaiah's Emmanuel was in fact Jesus, and therefore that Jesus had to have been virgin born to fulfill prophecy. And that one supposition changed the course of Christianity.

Regardless of the origin of the virgin birth idea, and Matthew's use of it when writing his Gospel around the year 85, it served two purposes: It made the Christian faith palatable to pagan converts, who had been taught about virgin births in their former religions.[19] And it captured the transcendent dimensions of God in the words and concepts that were available and understandable in the first century.

Paul's letters

Paul does not mention a miraculous virgin birth anywhere in his writings. On the contrary, he seems to think that Jesus' birth was natural and conventional. In Galatians he says this:

> But when the fullness of time had come, God sent his Son, *born of a woman...*[20]

Here, he means that Jesus' birth was ordinary. "There is no allusion here to the miraculous conception."[21]

A few years later, Paul makes his only other reference to Jesus' birth:

> ...the gospel concerning [God's] Son, *who was descended from David* according to the flesh...[22]

The phrase "descended from David" suggests that Paul believes Jesus to be the son of *Joseph*, who was descended from David. And "according to the flesh" implies a natural birth like any other.[23]

The "necessity" of the virgin birth

Some people argue for the virgin birth of Jesus on the grounds that it is a logical necessity. It is needed to support other church doctrines, including Original Sin. They point out that without the virgin birth, Jesus would have inherited a sinful nature. And that would have prevented him from being the pure sacrifice that could "take away the sins" of the world.

The logic here is that Jesus obviously was virgin born because it would *later* be important to church doctrines created by councils of bishops. How ludicrous!

And furthermore, the essence of this argument seems to be that God is so powerful that He could arrange a virgin birth, but so weak that he couldn't simply protect a conventionally born Jesus from "Adam's curse." How absurd!

What did Jesus think?

According to the Gospel accounts, Jesus never mentioned being born miraculously of a virgin. If he had come into the world in an entirely unique way, then it would have been the most important event in human history up to that point, with respect to salvation. And Jesus certainly wouldn't have kept it a secret. He obviously would have told people about it.

What's interesting about Jesus is not how he came into the *world*, but how he came into the *kingdom*. He did it day by day, choice by choice, prayer by prayer. With each healing word, with each act of kindness, with each expression of goodwill, he grew into what people believed him to be. And he wanted everyone to enter God's kingdom in the same way he did—one step at a time.

Conclusion

The entire case for the virgin birth seems to lie in one man's interpretation of an 800-year old prediction. If the writer of Matthew had not "connected the dots" in a particular way, it's unlikely that the idea of virgin birth would have taken hold in the early Christian community.

But Matthew's Bible was the Septuagint. And what he read in it was not the correct "the young woman shall conceive and bear a son," but the incorrect "the virgin shall conceive and bear a son." So his conclusion that Jesus was virgin born was based on an unfortunate mistranslation.

Jesus never once mentioned that he was miraculously conceived and born of a virgin. Nor did he act as if that were the case. He was *a part* of the human community, not *apart* from it. And he transformed lives—and transforms them today—not because of a unique type of birth, but because of a unique intensity of faith, hope, and love.

Was Jesus fully human and at the same time fully God?

Traditional Christianity sees Jesus as a unique person with two natures:

> "...the divine and human natures of Jesus do not exist beside one another in an unconnected way but rather are joined in him in a personal unity that has traditionally been referred to as the hypostatic union."[24]

This view, although widely held today, was not easily established. Early on there were alternative views, summarized succinctly by theologian Israel Steinmetz:

> "They either deny the genuineness (Ebionism) or the completeness (Arianism) of Jesus' deity, deny the genuineness (Docetism) or the completeness (Apollinarianism) of his humanity, divide his person (Nestorianism), or confuse his natures (Eutychianism)."[25]

It wasn't until 451, at the Council of Chalcedon, that Jesus was determined to have two natures. There, the 500 or so attendees decided that Jesus was simultaneously "truly God and truly man."[26] And thus the incomprehensible "dual nature" doctrine was established as something that must, *for the rest of time*, be believed by Christians without question.

Did Jesus' disciples think he had two natures?

We know what the Christians in leadership roles thought in the year 451. But what about 420 years or so earlier? What did those who would spread the new faith—Jesus' disciples—think?

According to Harry Emerson Fosdick, they

> "...were swept off their feet, fascinated by a personality whom they could not resist, convinced that something new, prophetic, was happening in Israel..." And they, at various times, interpreted Jesus as "...God's prophet, God's Son,

God's suffering servant, and God's coming
victorious Son of Man."[27]

But those who knew Jesus best never talked about him as
a person with two completely different natures.

Problems with the traditional view

Having Jesus be divine and human at the same time presents some logical difficulties, as many writers have noted. In
particular, it is at odds with the law of noncontradiction,
which Aristotle thought of as "the most certain principle." It
states that "...nothing can both be and not be at the same time
and in the same respect..."[28]

Furthermore, the traditional view, with Jesus as truly God
and truly human, forces us to twist the meanings of words.
For example, if Jesus could not sin, then being truly human
really means being *somewhat* truly human. And if he lacked
knowledge in some areas, then being truly God means being
somewhat truly God.

Some people, realizing the difficulty of explaining in a convincing way the idea of dual natures, simply give up and
declare that it is a mystery beyond human understanding. But
that's not an argument. As one writer astutely points out,
"mystery is the last refuge of a befuddled theologian."[29]

Support for the dual-nature idea

Those who argue that Jesus was both fully human and fully divine will typically cite passages such as this one written
by the Apostle Peter:

...To those who have received a faith as precious
as ours through the righteousness of our God
and Savior Jesus Christ:[30]

But statements like this one do not unambiguously convey the idea of a "hypostatic union" of divine and human natures. And "our God and Savior" could simply be like my saying "my niece and nephew." I wouldn't be implying that they were the same person.

On the other hand, Jesus is clearly identified as an ordinary man in a variety of verses. For example:

> ...Jesus of Nazareth, a man attested to you by God
> with deeds of power, wonders, and signs that
> God did through him among you...[31]

So some New Testament writers saw Jesus as simply a gifted man, and some saw him as much more. But I couldn't find a clear indication that any of them saw him as a person with two incompatible natures, one completely human and one completely divine.

What did Jesus think?

Jesus never talked about coming from heaven to earth, forming a unique God-man. He *did* stand out from the crowd: he knew things that others didn't, and he could do things that others couldn't. But he didn't attribute his abilities to a unique dual nature.

John's Jesus is the exception. In the Fourth Gospel, Jesus is presented as making a variety of grandiose claims:

> "I am the gate. Whoever enters by me will be
> saved..."[32]

> "The Father and I are one."[33]

> "...I am the way, and the truth, and the life..."[34]

But these sayings are very likely not authentic because they don't align with what we see in Mark, Matthew, and Luke. "Jesus' self-interpretation as given in the Fourth Gospel cannot be integrated with the self-interpretation we find in the Synoptic Gospels."[35]

Jesus didn't tell people that he represented a unique and mysterious union of divine and human natures. It's hard to imagine him complicating things like that. Instead, he kept it simple and *showed* people what divinity looked like in human interactions: he acted with compassion; he extended goodwill to all; he helped those in need, regardless of their status.

There was nothing supernatural going on—just someone aligning himself with divine purpose to achieve extraordinary results.

Conclusion

The idea that Jesus was both fully human and fully God was not something that his followers believed. The written accounts make it clear that, although they thought that Jesus was remarkable, they didn't think of him as eternal God in a temporary body.

The idea that Jesus represented a unique union of God and man was put forth at the Council of Chalcedon more than *four hundred years* after Jesus. It was there that the idea of "truly God and truly man" was declared to be the only acceptable way of viewing Jesus.

Jesus himself never claimed to be a unique God-man. He knew, of course, that others considered him to be exceptional. But he didn't intend for people to merely observe him and be filled with wonder. He intended for them to emulate him. So whatever divine nature Jesus possessed, it had to be the same one that we all possess to some extent.

Is the traditional view of incarnation the most useful one?

Many in the Christian community feel that the traditional view of incarnation, with God the Son entering the world in the man Jesus, is the only suitable way to understand the idea. But is this view really the best way of thinking about incarnation? Is it the most useful way of framing the idea that God is active in human affairs?

Problems with the traditional view

I think that the traditional view of incarnation presents two problems that need to be considered.

First, it minimizes the accomplishments of Jesus. If he was the unique God-man, then nothing was ever difficult or in doubt. Convincing people to repent? Easy. Healing those who were hurting? Easy. Resisting temptation? Easy. Whatever he did as God-man, it was unremarkable because he always had limitless power and wisdom on which to draw.

The other problem with this concept of incarnation is that I can only observe and acknowledge it. I can't play any role in it because I don't represent a "hypostatic union" of human and divine natures. So it's merely something that I must accept and believe, and yet get no practical benefit from in my daily life.

Any views of incarnation that overcome these problems would, in my opinion, be worth looking at.

Is incarnation a one-time event?

Theologian R. C. Sproul describes the Incarnation as

> "...the supreme moment of visitation of the eternal with the temporal, the infinite with the finite, the unconditioned with the conditioned."[36]

But did incarnation occur at a particular moment? Or does it occur even now? Some have speculated that incarnation can best be viewed as a process rather than as an event. Here are just a few ideas that have been advanced over the years.

Isaac Dorner, a nineteenth century German Lutheran, offered a theory of progressive incarnation. His view was that Jesus was not the God-man from the beginning, but "as Jesus yielded to the Father in all things, the Logos gradually penetrated His humanity."[37]

Philosopher Alfred North Whitehead thought that God is present in every moment of experience. His idea was that we all are, to some extent, incarnations of divine wisdom and creativity. And the "greater openness toward God's presence in our lives, the more God can be present, guiding, energizing, and inspiring our lives."[38]

Psychologist Carl Jung, in the 1950s, put forth his idea of progressive incarnation:

> "The continuing direct operation of the Holy
> [Spirit] on those who are called to be God's
> children implies, in fact, a broadening process of
> incarnation. Christ...is the first-born who is suc-
> ceeded by an ever-increasing number of young-
> er brothers and sisters."[39]

And more recently, pastor Chuck Queen described incarnation as a process:

> "...incarnation is not a once-for-all single event; it
> is ongoing. When Jesus says, 'As the Father sent
> me, so I send you,' he is charging us, his follow-
> ers, with the responsibility and privilege of
> carrying forward this process, of continuing this
> movement of incarnating God tangibly and
> materially, in human life—in human relation-
> ships and interactions."[40]

So the traditional view of incarnation is not the only view. It is old and familiar, but that doesn't mean that we must accept it without question, nor that it must be the most helpful way of thinking about the topic.

What did Jesus think?

Jesus never said anything consistent with what would 400 years later become carved-in-stone church doctrine. He never said anything to suggest that he believed God became involved in human affairs at one and only one time in one and only one person.

But his teachings are consistent with the idea that incarnation is a *process* in which we all can become involved. Consider how he encouraged people to pray:

> "Your kingdom come. Your will be done, on earth
> as it is in heaven."[41]

Jesus obviously was referring to something that couldn't happen suddenly. Such a change would have to take place gradually, over time, as we become more receptive to God's presence and influence in our lives.

And consider what he said to people who wanted to live as he lived:

> ..."If any want to become my followers, let them
> deny themselves and take up their cross and
> follow me."[42]

Again, he was talking about something that happens over time. To follow Jesus means learning to accept that God is revealing Himself in us the way He revealed Himself in Jesus—gradually. Jesus, during his life, became "poor in spirit" and day by day aligned himself more and more with divine purpose. And he seemed to say that we all could do the same.

So although Jesus didn't talk about incarnation *per se*, his ideas align with the notion of ongoing, gradual incarnation. He clearly understood that God enters human affairs *as we allow ourselves to feel His presence and influence*. As Ken Pennings puts it, "In each one of us, human as we are, the one true God is potentially revealed and encountered."[43]

Conclusion

The traditional view of incarnation—that the second person of a holy trinity formed a unique union with the man Jesus—is just one way of interpreting the idea. And it's one that has some drawbacks. For example, it makes all of Jesus' accomplishments unremarkable because he always had infinite resources on which to draw. And it makes all of us mere observers.

Some have suggested that incarnation could better be thought of as a natural process rather than a supernatural event. In this way, God-with-us takes on a new and personal dimension.

Jesus never taught anything that is consistent with the traditional view of incarnation. He didn't identify himself as the one and only God incarnate, even though that would have been a powerful motivator for those who would start the Christian movement. He did, however, put forth ideas consistent with an understanding of incarnation as an ongoing process. He clearly knew that the more receptive we become to God's revelation in us and though us, the more it happens.

Summary

A few years ago, the only thing I knew about incarnation was what I had heard countless times. I didn't know when the concept originated, how it developed, or how it became doctrine. But ignorance gradually gave way to enlightenment, and I now have a better understanding of the idea and its true significance.

Update to what I know

I now know that incarnation as we understand it today is not a biblical idea. Jesus didn't teach it, nor did Paul. And the

Gospel writers, although presenting Jesus as someone special—messiah, savior, *logos*—did not identify him as a unique union of God and man. That idea wasn't put forth until the mid fifth century. Then, at the Council of Chalcedon, bishops decreed that Jesus, and only Jesus, must be seen as "truly God and truly man."

Judging from what Jesus did and did not say, I don't think that he saw himself as the one and only God-man. He never said anything about being miraculously conceived and born of a virgin. Nor did he live as if he were fundamentally different from others. But he was certainly unique in his ability to demonstrate what divinity looks like in the world. He took ordinary love and compassion and concern to extraordinary levels.

Jesus gradually embraced the God within, and lived in a way that inspired others. But he clearly believed that we all could do the same. His view, that God's kingdom can come "on earth as it is in heaven," is a clear indication that he thought of incarnation as an ongoing process. And we all can become involved in it.

Course change

Based on what I've discovered, I have decided to give up the traditional church view of incarnation and instead to follow Jesus. Although he recognized that he had a divine nature, he unquestionably believed that everyone else did as well. He knew that whatever divinity he possessed, it was the same that others could possess—if they chose to do so. We all are part of God's family, and can help in establishing His kingdom.

Jesus' teachings are consistent with the idea that God enters the world not one time, but countless times, becoming incarnate in each individual. He gives each person the opportunity to become His voice and hands in human affairs. I think that this makes sense and aligns with actual experience.

So the traditional view—that incarnation is a one-time event involving a supernatural act—is no longer very appealing. My Christian faith no longer depends on incarnation being a particular type of *event*. It depends on Jesus being a particular type of *individual:* someone who seemed to believe that God, through a natural process, can become incarnate in all people, and that we can become receptive to His presence and influence. Thus incarnation is no longer something that I merely accept and believe. Instead, it is a dynamic process in which I can *participate*. What a powerful and motivational perspective!

Notes

[1] "Incarnation." *Merriam-Webster Dictionary*,
https://www.merriam-webster.com/dictionary/incarnation
[2] "Incarnation." *Internet Encyclopedia of Philosophy*,
https://www.iep.utm.edu/incarnat/
[3] "Incarnation: Jesus Christ." *Encyclopaedia Britannica*,
https://www.britannica.com/topic/Incarnation-Jesus-Christ
[4] Cohen, Caleb. "How to Explain the Incarnation to Hindus." International Mission Board, 2018,
https://www.imb.org/2018/12/19/explain-incarnation-hindus/
[5] Achtemeier, Paul J., ed. "Incarnation." *The HarperCollins Bible Dictionary*. San Francisco: HarperOne, 1996.
[6] Galatians 4:4
[7] Philippians 2:5-6
[8] "Philippians 2:5-11 'Let the same mind be in you that was in Christ Jesus...'" Unity, Unity Worldwide Ministries,
http://www.unity.org/resources/bible-interpretation/philippians-25-11-let-same-mind-be-you-was-christ-jesus

[9] John 1:1, 14

[10] *Collins Dictionary.* "Logos,"
https://www.collinsdictionary.com/us/dictionary/english/logos

[11] Jones, Victoria Emily. "Jesus as Logos, or Cosmic Christ (Part 1)." The Jesus Question, 2011,
https://thejesusquestion.org/2011/03/07/jesus-as-logos-or-cosmic-christ-part-1/

[12] Matthew 17:20

[13] Matthew 5:14

[14] Pearce, Jonathan M. S. "Debunking the Nativity: The Virgin Birth." Patheos, 2016,
https://www.patheos.com/blogs/tippling/2016/12/05/debunking-nativity-virgin-birth/

[15] Burke, Daniel. "Did Isaiah Really Predict the Virgin Birth?" Washington Post, 2012,
https://www.washingtonpost.com/national/on-faith/did-isaiah-really-predict-the-virgin-birth/2012/12/12/fe809baa-44a8-11e2-8c8f-fbebf7ccab4e_story.html

[16] Matthew 1:21

[17] Matthew 1:22-23

[18] Bratcher, Dennis. "Isaiah 7:14: Translation Issues." *The Voice*, Christian Resource Institute, 2018,
http://www.crivoice.org/isa7-14.html

[19] "The Virgin Birth (Conception) of Jesus." Religious Tolerance, Religious Tolerance.
http://www.religioustolerance.org/virgin_b1.htm

[20] Galatians 4:4

[21] *Ellicott's Commentary for English Readers.* Bible Hub,
https://biblehub.com/commentaries/ellicott/galatians/4.htm

[22] Romans 1:3

[23] "The Virgin Birth (Conception) of Jesus." Religious Tolerance,
http://www.religioustolerance.org/virgin_b1.htm
[24] "Incarnation: Jesus Christ." *Encyclopaeda Britannica*,
https://www.britannica.com/topic/Incarnation-Jesus-Christ
[25] Steinmetz, Israel. "The Doctrine of the Incarnation: A Historical Exploration – Part 3." *Artios Magazine*, LifeSpring School of Ministry, 2018,
https://artiosmagazine.org/god-thoughts/doctrine-incarnation-part-3/
[26] "The Chalcedonian Creed Circa 451 A.D." *A Puritan's Mind*, Puritan Publications,
http://www.apuritansmind.com/creeds-and-confessions/the-chalcedonian-creed-circa-451-a-d/
[27] Fosdick, Harry Emerson. *The Man From Nazareth*. New York: Harper & Brothers, 1949, pp. 165, 184.
[28] Feiser, James, and Dowden, Bradley, eds. "Incarnation." *Internet Encyclopedia of Philosophy,*
https://www.iep.utm.edu/incarnat/
[29] Fakhoury, Gary. "The Incarnation: Does It Make Sense?" The Bible Unitarian,
http://thebibleunitarian.org/articles/christology/the-incarnation-does-it-make-sense
[30] 2 Peter 1:1
[31] Acts 2:22
[32] John 10:9
[33] John 10:30
[34] John 14:6
[35] Williams, Daniel Day. "Chapter 8: The Incarnation." *The Spirit and the Forms of Love*. Religion Online,
https://www.religion-online.org/book-chapter/chapter-8-the-incarnation/

[36] Sproul, R. C. "Interpreting the Logos." Crosswalk, 2014, https://www.crosswalk.com/devotionals/inpresenceofgod/in-the-presence-of-god-week-of-april-12-11628730.html

[37] Amsterdam, Peter. "The Heart of It All: The Incarnation (Part 3)." *Directors' Corner*, The Family International, 2011, https://directors.tfionline.com/post/heart-it-all-incarnation-part-3/

[38] Epperly, Bruce. "Why We Need an Incarnation: A Progressive Vision." Patheos, 2011, https://www.patheos.com/blogs/faithforward/2011/12/why-we-need-an-incarnation-a-progressive-vision/

[39] Jung, Carl. *Answer to Job*. New York: Bollingen Foundation, 1958, chapter 658, https://books.google.com/books?id=by-aWKndzRkC&printsec=frontcover&source=gbs_atb#v=onepage&q&f=false

[40] Queen, Chuck. "God Incarnate In Us (John 20:19-23)." Progressive Christianity, 2014, https://progressivechristianity.org/resources/god-incarnate-in-us-john-2019-23/

[41] Matthew 6:10

[42] Matthew 16:24

[43] Pennings, Ken. "Incarnation—in What Respect is Jesus the God-man?" Orchard Ridge United Church of Christ, 2019, https://www.orucc.org/incarnation-in-what-respect-is-jesus-the-god-man-ken-pennings-6-23-2019/

3. Atonement

Introduction

Atonement is generally understood to mean "amends or reparation made for an injury or wrong."[1] But in the world of faith, it more precisely means the reconciliation of humans with God, which is made necessary by the fact that humans are imperfect. Our imperfection results in sin, which is incompatible with God's holiness. Thus there is a need for atonement to restore the broken relationship and experience true fellowship with God.

Atonement is not unique to the Christian faith. It is a recurring theme in the history of religion. Rituals to make amends and please God "...appear in most religions...as the means by which the religious person reestablishes or strengthens his relation to the holy or divine."[2]

In Judaism, for example, individuals seek to attain God's forgiveness for sins in various ways, including repentance, payment for a wrong action, good works, suffering, and prayer. And in Islam, a five-step method is used:

"One, to admit that what you've done is wrong; two, to detest it in your heart; three, to commit to turn away from it and not to go back; four, to make restitution; and then five, to ask for God's forgiveness."[3]

But in Christianity, atonement is the central theme, and Jesus of Nazareth is the central figure. The idea that he, in some way, facilitates the uniting of humans with God is the fundamental message of the faith. But exactly how and why it happens has been hotly debated for the past two thousand years. And even today there are many different views about atonement within the Christian community.

Conventional view

The conventional Christian view is that the first humans rebelled against God, separating themselves, and all people since, from God. The result of our sinful nature is spiritual death, which is deserved because God abhors sin. The divine-human chasm is so wide that we cannot bridge it and save ourselves. But Jesus, acting in a superhuman way, took our punishment, died for our sins, and effectively absorbed God's wrath.

I began reading about the ideas expressed and implied in this conventional view to see if they were justified, reasonable, and essential to my Christian faith. I was curious about how they originated, how they evolved, and why they are widely embraced.

In this chapter, I'll discuss some of the questions I've asked about atonement, and also the unexpected answers that have helped me to gain a better understanding of the idea.

Are we naturally corrupt and sinful?

One widely held view in the Christian community is that we are, by nature, sinful. And growing up in a Baptist church, I heard that message loud and clear each week. How did I know that I was naturally sinful? Because Paul says so in his letter to the Christians in Rome:

> ...all have sinned and fall short of the glory of God.[4]

Furthermore, I learned (again from Paul) that sin has dire consequences:

> For the wages of sin is death...[5]

I wondered why I, a small boy living in a small town, was in such trouble. The reason? Adam and Eve disobeyed God and brought sin into the world, thereby altering the human condition. And everyone who followed necessarily had a sinful nature—or as *The Catholic Encyclopedia* picturesquely puts it, "the hereditary stain."[6]

(But, as I found out a few years ago, the idea that we inherit a sinful nature was largely the invention of Augustine of Hippo, the fourth century philosopher we met in Chapter 1. He took the Genesis story of the first humans' disobedience to God and turned it into a *curse* that is passed along biologically via sexual union. This is what people today mean when they use the term "original sin.")[7]

Furthermore, I learned (once again from Paul) that I was powerless against my sinfulness:

> For while we were still weak, at the right time Christ died for the ungodly.[8]

Many believe that these three ideas offered by Paul form the foundation of atonement. Christian writer J. Warner Wallace sums it up this way:

> "If you don't understand your true condition,
> your fallen nature, and the inability of your own
> efforts to save yourself, you won't move to seek
> and find the Savior who has come to give us
> what we simply can't earn on our own."[9]

But is that true? Is the essence of atonement found in the depressing condition of being fallen, condemned, and helpless? The writer of Genesis certainly never said he thought that we enter the world in such a condition. But he did imagine our origins in a positive and inspiring way —which many Christians over the centuries have chosen to ignore. He opined that:

> • God placed us in a garden—*thus He loves us*.
>
> • God gave us the responsibility for tending the garden—*thus He trusts us*.
>
> • God created us in his image, thereby endowing us with creative ability so we can make changes to the garden—*thus He empowers us*.[10]

So the actual biblical account has us entering the world in a *blessed* state, not a *wretched* state. But that doesn't mean atonement isn't a necessary and worthwhile pursuit.

What did Jesus think?

Jesus obviously acknowledged the capacity of humans to engage in evil, self destruction, and other counterproductive acts:

> "For it is from within, from the human heart, that evil intentions come: fornication, theft, murder, adultery, avarice, wickedness, deceit, licentiousness, envy, slander, pride, folly. All these evil things come from within, and they defile a person..."[11]

Here, what many Christians *wish* Jesus had said is: "...All these evil things come from Adam and Eve by way of inherited sin, and your very *nature* defiles you." That would make the doctrine of Original Sin, and the notion that we are naturally corrupt, look very interesting indeed.

But that's not what he said at all. Jesus made his point of view clear: Evil comes from within the individual by choice, and that type of choice is what corrupts one's purity. That is what puts distance between us and God.

On another occasion, Jesus spoke against the idea of a sinful nature in a different way:

> "Truly I tell you, whoever does not receive the kingdom of God *as a little child* will never enter it."[12]

If we were born corrupt, then there would be no value in becoming, spiritually, like a child. It wouldn't get us any closer to the kingdom of God. So Jesus clearly believed that we are not sinful by nature. He urged people to return to their natural blessed state so they could draw nearer to God.

And at another time, Jesus speculated about our true nature with this comment:

> "You are the light of the world..."[13]

If he thought that we were tainted with a sinful and corrupt nature, it seems like he would have declared us to be the "darkness of the world." But that's not what he said. It would have been inconsistent with his belief that we all are members of God's family.

Jesus did, however, recognize the need to do something about the bad choices that separate us from God. How did he propose that we—*we*, not God—close the gap? He stressed that repenting (acknowledging mistakes and deciding to turn away from them) was essential and effective:

> "...there will be more joy in heaven over one
> sinner who repents than over ninety-nine
> righteous persons who need no repentance."[14]

Why would there be such joy if sincere repentance did not serve to reconcile, to atone, to draw us closer to God? Jesus clearly believed that confession and repentance could bring about an inward transformation that effectively bridges the divine-human gap created by ungodly thoughts and actions.

Jesus didn't teach that a sinful nature is passed from one generation to the next. Instead, he focused on personal responsibility when it came to sin and its consequences. His views of human nature and atonement seem to fit with the interpretation of the Genesis creation narrative that I put forth earlier. He obviously didn't think that we come into the world as maladjusted creatures who offend the One who created us. His message was consistent with the idea that we come into the world as the loved, trusted, and empowered children of God.

Conclusion

The writer of Genesis gave an account of creation in which the first humans disobeyed God, and then realized that such disobedience has consequences. But the idea that human nature abruptly changed at that moment, and became for all time corrupt, is not found in the story. And besides, if biology is on the right track, then the real trajectory of the human family since our creation has not been downward but upward.

But the Bible's writers do make it abundantly clear that we all tend to make choices that are not in the best interests of ourselves or our neighbors. We sometimes allow base motives to guide us. And in doing so, we distance ourselves from God. So the need to atone, to reunite,

to reconcile, is real for those who desire to grow spiritually and live abundantly.

Jesus understood that sin was not at the core of human
nature. He taught that we are born into God's family with
great capacity to live righteous and moral lives. He encouraged people to be motivated by their higher instincts:
to love God, themselves, and their neighbors; to align
themselves with divine purpose; to harness the power of
prayer in their daily lives. He made it clear that what's
important is not dwelling on our human *nature*, but tap-
ping into our human *potential*.

Is God wrathful?

The idea that God is wrathful has been embraced by a
great many Christians for quite a long time. The logic goes
like this: We sin; God abhors sin; hence the wrath.

Jonathan Edwards, the eighteenth century Colonial
American preacher, drove home the idea with fiery sermons full of vivid imagery. Here's an example from "Sinners in the Hands of an Angry God":

> "The bow of God's wrath is bent with the arrow
> ready on the string. Justice aims the arrow at
> your heart, straining the bow. It is nothing but
> the mere pleasure of God that prohibits, for even
> one moment, the arrow from becoming drunk on
> your blood."[15]

Perhaps Pastor Edwards had been inspired by the
words of the prophet Nahum, who some 2000 years earlier shared his conception of God:

> A jealous and avenging God is the Lord, the Lord
> is avenging and wrathful...[16]

Of course the idea that God is full of wrath, and could "pour it out" on deserving sinners at any time, originated long before Nahum came along. In looking through the Old Testament, I came across example after example in which writers give accounts of God's wrathful responses to human activity that offends Him.

Sometimes God directed his wrath at individuals:

> Now Aaron's sons, Nadab and Abihu, each took
> his censer, put fire in it, and laid incense on it;
> and they offered unholy fire before the Lord,
> such as he had not commanded them. And fire
> came out from the presence of the Lord and
> consumed them, and they died before the Lord.[17]

And sometimes God directed his wrath at large groups of people:

> Then the Lord rained on Sodom and Gomorrah
> sulfur and fire from the Lord out of heaven; and
> he overthrew those cities, and all the Plain, and
> all the inhabitants of the cities, and what grew
> on the ground.[18]

But these examples, and all others, pale when compared with the great flood, during which God reportedly unleashed His wrath to an astounding degree:

> So the Lord said, "I will blot out from the earth
> the human beings I have created—people [about
> *20 million* men, women, and children] together
> with animals and creeping things and birds of
> the air, for I am sorry that I have made them."[19]

It's no wonder that the ancient Jewish people tried to appease God with sacrifices and rituals. Avoiding God's wrath was essential to survival. And it needed to happen frequently. According to one count, God shows his wrath in the Bible 499 times![20]

And it's not just in the Old Testament that we find God portrayed as wrathful. For example, Paul, in his letter to the Roman Christians, says this:

> ...for those who are self-seeking and who obey not the truth but wickedness, there will be wrath and fury.[21]

Some have attempted to define "wrath" so it's not so frightening and antithetical to a loving a merciful God. For example, evangelical pastor Colin Smith put it this way: "God's wrath is the just and measured response of his holiness toward evil."[22]

Regardless of the exact nature of wrath, an obvious question comes to mind: Is God really filled with wrath? And if so, does that imply that He needs to, or wants to, express that wrath in a way that affects me personally?

What did Jesus think?

Jesus didn't encourage people to be motivated out of fear of God's wrath, but out of desire to be part of His family:

> "Do not be afraid, little flock, for it is your Father's good pleasure to give you the kingdom."[23]

What a remarkable and reassuring statement that many Christians choose to ignore! Jesus was making it clear that we should seek the kingdom not because God would otherwise punish us, but because He wants what is best for us.

Jesus was knowledgeable about Scripture, so he surely understood the ancient and primitive view of God as wrathful. But he didn't feel compelled to perpetuate that idea just because it was familiar and widely accepted. He put forth a more mature view. Jesus' God was not angry, intolerant, and punishing. He was generous, merciful, and loving—a view that's apparent in his parable of the Prodigal Son.[24]

Seeing God with such positive characteristics wasn't entirely new. A thousand years earlier, a psalmist wrote these comforting words:

> The Lord is my shepherd, I shall not want.[25]

But Jesus gave the idea a practical spin, suggesting that God valued each and every lost soul. Thus "a new day in mankind's spiritual history began."[26]

Jesus' disciples believed that they saw in their master the qualities of God—not omniscience or omnipotence, of course, but an extraordinary measure of mercy, patience, love, and kindness. It's interesting that they didn't see in him wrath that destroyed or degraded individuals who were less than righteous.

Jesus did, however, speak of God's *judgment:*

> Every tree that does not bear good fruit is cut down and thrown into the fire.[27]

> For with the judgment you make you will be judged, and the measure you give will be the measure you get.[28]

But Jesus never used the idea of a wrathful God to influence people. He obviously recognized that motivating individuals with fear would not produce the real change of heart needed for people to enter the kingdom and experience fellowship with God.

Conclusion

The idea that God is wrathful is found throughout the Old Testament writings. Again and again we see God expressing his righteous anger in a variety of ways: mass killings, plagues, curses, floods. And sometimes He does it in more creative ways, such as turning someone into a block of salt.[29] But the message was clear: God is to be feared, and avoiding His punishment is the key to survival.

The value of such accounts is that they make it clear that ungodly thoughts and actions have consequences. The early Jewish people imagined that these consequences—often discomfort or pain—were directly administered by a wrathful God. But in fact they were administered dispassionately by a lawful universe. When we think and act in ways that aren't in alignment with divine purpose, when we get "out of synch" with spiritual laws, we likely will experience negative consequences.

Jesus didn't promote the ancient idea of a wrathful God. His God was kind, patient, and compassionate. So he didn't try to motivate people to *avoid* something dreadful (God's wrath), but to *approach* something wonderful (God's love and mercy). And he emphasized the critical role of repentance, which can bring about true inward transformation. The result is a renewed awareness of our place in God's family. And that can give us confidence to enter the kingdom and draw closer to God.

Are humans powerless against sin?

Many in the Christian community are convinced that the gap between humans and God is so vast that it cannot be bridged by human efforts. This view is tied to the "sinful nature" idea: because we, with our inherited sinfulness, have created the problem, we can't also create the solution.

The Bible verse that people love to point to was written by—you guessed it—Paul. In his letter to the Christians at Ephesus, he writes:

> For by grace you have been saved through faith,
> and this is not your own doing; it is the gift of
> God—not the result of works, so that no one may
> boast.[30]

This notion of personal ineffectiveness in atonement has been exalted over the centuries by inclusion in various formal declarations of faith. For example, in the 1530 *Augsburg Confession*, we find this in Article XX:

> First, that our works cannot reconcile God or
> merit forgiveness of sins, grace, and justification,
> but that we obtain this only by faith when we
> believe that we are received into favor for
> Christ's sake...[31]

And in the 1689 *Baptist Confession of Faith*, Chapter 9, we find this:

> Man, by his fall into a state of sin, hath wholly
> lost all ability of will to any spiritual good ac-
> companying salvation; so as a natural man, being
> altogether averse from that good, and dead in
> sin, is not able by his own strength to convert
> himself, or to prepare himself thereunto.[32]

And recently, a Baptist pastor stated it a bit more suc-cinctly: "We're all helpless in our own strength..."[33]

But the idea that we are powerless to bridge the divine-human gap is relatively new. All throughout the Old Tes-tament, we see the Jewish people taking responsibility for their sins and attempting to reconcile with God. They used sacrifices, rituals, prayer, repentance, and obedience to the law to make amends. Paul himself thought that salvation "had once [before Christ] been attainable through ad-herence to the system of Jewish laws in the Hebrew Scrip-tures..."[34]

> Now before faith came, we were imprisoned and
> guarded under the law until faith would be re-
> vealed. Therefore the law was our disciplinarian
> until Christ came, so that we might be justified
> by faith.[35]

So the view that humans are powerless against sin
seems to be primarily a New Testament idea—but it's not
one found in the Gospels. This is interesting because some
of Paul's writings had been circulating for a dozen years or
so before Mark, the first Gospel account, was written.[36]

What did Jesus think?

Jesus did not teach that we are helpless against sinfulness. He repeatedly stressed that our spiritual quality is
under our control:

> "Enter through the narrow gate; for the gate is
> wide and the road is easy that leads to destruc-
> tion, and there are many who take it. For the
> gate is narrow and the road is hard that leads to
> life, and there are few who find it."[37]

The obvious implications here are that: a) we can dis-
cern the desirable path from the undesirable one; and b)
we have the power to choose which path we follow. One
increases our distance from God, while the other decreas-
es it (that is, helps to achieve atonement).

Jesus didn't say much about human weakness. But he
did talk a lot about human power. He stressed the extraordinary capabilities of ordinary people. He believed
that we all have the capacity to lift ourselves to a higher
plane. He thought that we can, if we choose to, act in ways
that contrast sharply with sinfulness.

For example, Jesus thought that we could love our enemies rather than hate them:

> "But love your enemies, do good, and lend,
> expecting nothing in return..."[38]

He thought that we could eliminate hypocrisy:

> "...how can you say to your neighbor, 'Let me
> take the speck out of your eye,' while the log is in
> your own eye? You hypocrite, first take the log
> out of your own eye, and then you will see clear-
> ly to take the speck out of your neighbor's eye."[39]

He thought that we could replace hardness of heart with mercy and compassion—something he emphasized with the Good Samaritan parable.[40]

And Jesus also thought that we could overcome the tendency to condemn and seek vengeance:

> "[Forgive] not seven times, but, I tell you,
> seventy-seven times."[41]

If Jesus thought that we were helpless against sinfulness, he wouldn't have encouraged people to overcome it. But he continually stressed personal responsibility and personal power with regard to sin. He challenged people to turn from evil, ignore destructive impulses, and grasp fully the meaning of being part of God's family.

Conclusion

Throughout human history, people have taken an active role in their salvation and have tried to please God in various ways, for example, by being obedient to the law. And even Paul thought that to be effective—but only until Jesus came along. The new way of achieving reconciliation with God, in Paul's view, was by holding a particular belief:

> ...if you confess with your lips that Jesus is Lord
> and believe in your heart that God raised him
> from the dead, you will be saved.[42]

In an attempt to show the necessity of Jesus' sacrifice, Paul stressed the ineffectiveness of human efforts in bringing about atonement. Thus began the great debate about whether faith alone is sufficient for receiving God's grace, or whether "works" are essential as well. The debate came into focus during the Reformation, during which Martin Luther promoted the "faith alone" point of view. But as far as I know, the question has not yet been settled to everyone's satisfaction.

Jesus' approach to atonement was more pragmatic. He encouraged people to understand the power they had to control their distance from God. They could choose to be motivated by base instincts such as greed, selfishness, envy, and lust. Or they could choose to be motivated by higher instincts, such as generosity, service, compassion, and love. Jesus didn't teach people that atonement would come about *later* without their involvement. He taught that atonement could come about *now*, and that it was the responsibility of each individual to pursue it. He emphasized that the kingdom was at hand, and that repentance was the key that opened its doors (or in other words, the means for reconciliation).[43]

Was Jesus punished in my place for my sins?

If you asked a group of Christians to sum up the good news in a few words, I think most would say, "Jesus died for my sins." The consequence, they would add, is that they are saved (from eternal punishment for having a sinful nature) because Jesus took the punishment that they deserved.

I always thought that this was the only suitable way of thinking about atonement in the Christian faith. So imagine my surprise, decades later, to discover that it—

called Penal Substitution—is just one of many ways of looking at the topic.

Detailed accounts of the traditional theories of atonement are easy to find,[44] so I'll give the briefest of overviews here:

> • *Ransom:* Jesus' death served as a ransom to Satan, thus satisfying the debt humans owe because of inherited sinfulness.

> • *Moral Influence:* Jesus' purpose was to bring about a positive change to humanity, inspiring people to live moral lives.

> • *Christus Victor:* Jesus' death on the cross defeated the powers of evil that hold humans in bondage, thus setting us free.

> • *Satisfaction:* Jesus' death satisfied God's need for justice regarding sin, which He must administer to restore His honor.

> • *Penal Substitution:* Jesus died to satisfy God's wrath against human sin, accepting the punishment deserved by all.

> • *Governmental:* Jesus died to accept *a* (not *my*) punishment to demonstrate God's revulsion at sin, and to regain His favor.

> • *Scapegoat:* Jesus, an innocent victim, was not offered to God, but *by* God to take away guilt, thereby demonstrating His love.

I discovered that the Ransom and Moral Influence theories were the first to be widely accepted. In fact, they dominated until the eleventh century, when Anselm of Canterbury proposed his Satisfaction theory. Penal Substitution theory, the one that many today insist that everyone *must* embrace, was not influential until the Reformation, some *1500 years* into the Christian era!

Nevertheless, Penal Substitution became more and more popular, and today is the dominant view. And at its core is the ancient and primitive belief that blood, released during a sacrifice, has the power to influence God.

What did Jesus think?

In my reading of the Gospels, I noticed that something was missing from Jesus' sayings: the word "atonement." Then I realized that it wasn't missing at all—Jesus just referred to it in an unusual way.

I think Jesus talked about atonement, about reconciliation, about drawing close to God, all the time. But in characteristic fashion, he went at it obliquely:

> "Blessed are the poor in spirit [those who cheerfully submit to divine will], for theirs is the kingdom of heaven."[45]

> "For I tell you, unless your righteousness exceeds that of the scribes and Pharisees, you will never enter the kingdom of heaven."[46]

> "Not everyone who says to me, 'Lord, Lord,' will enter the kingdom of heaven, but only the one who does the will of my Father in heaven."[47]

With these statements and others, Jesus made clear his belief that entering the kingdom—uniting with God—depends on our making certain choices. At no point does he say that he will open the door to the kingdom *for us*. At no point did Jesus say that our atonement was attainable only through *his* efforts.

In the Gospel of John, we do find this statement attributed to Jesus:

> ..."I am the way, and the truth, and the life. No
> one comes to the Father except through me."[48]

Proponents of Penal Substitution read "through me" to mean "through my upcoming sacrificial and bloody death on their behalf." But even if that is a reasonable interpretation, it probably doesn't matter. According to theologian John Hick, among mainline New Testament scholars "...there is today a general consensus that [the "I am" statements] are not pronouncements of the historical Jesus..."[49]

The "I am the way" statement is too uncharacteristic of the way Jesus thought about himself and expressed himself in the other Gospel accounts. It's also inconsistent with much of what he had to say regarding reconciliation in Mark, Matthew, and Luke. The book of John is not considered to be a historical record, but "an artistic theological masterpiece."[50] The author tries to express the love of God using words that he feels the Christians of his day need to hear Jesus say.

Some will point out that Jesus did say this:

> "For the Son of Man came not to be served but
> to serve, and to give his life as a ransom for
> many."[51]

But notice that he didn't say "to give *up* his life," but "to give his life," as one might give oneself devotedly to a cause or profession.

Others will refer to another "I am" statement in the Gospel of John:

> "I am the good shepherd. The good shepherd
> lays down his life for the sheep."[52]

But this statement, if authentic, isn't necessarily a prediction. It could be seen as a comment about how total commitment and selflessness are needed when serving others.

Those who believe in Penal Substitution see God's forgiveness as something that must be purchased with a bloody sacrifice. But it's instructive to consider what Jesus had to say about the matter:

> "Do not judge, and you will not be judged; do not condemn, and you will not be condemned. *Forgive, and you will be forgiven*."[53]

Unlike the "ransom" and "shepherd" verses, this one is straightforward and unambiguous. Jesus was saying that we make ourselves receptive to God's forgiveness simply by choosing forgiveness when we are offended by others. The significance of this idea is hard to overemphasize.

Conclusion

The notion that Jesus accepted the punishment meant for us, thereby making atonement possible, is a popular belief. But it has many flaws. First, it puts violence and retribution at the heart of the "Good News." Second, it reduces atonement to a legalistic transaction that doesn't require any significant change of heart. And third, it presents God as being limited, unable to extend his grace and mercy to us, His children, until He witnessed a particular barbaric act.

Penal Substitution has had proponents over the years, but Moral Influence and Ransom theories of atonement held sway for the first 1500 years of the Church. Only since the Reformation has punishment been placed at the center of atonement. Only since then had God been considered incapable of showing unbridled love for us until He was influenced by a bloody execution.

Jesus clearly understood that sin separates us from God, and that it is in our best interest that the gap be narrowed. But he stressed the importance of *accepting* responsibility rather than *shifting* responsibility. He taught that confession and repentance, with the inward transformation it made possible, get us into the kingdom of God. He implied that atonement is an ongoing *process* in which we play an active role, not a one-time *event* in which we play a passive role.

Summary

A few years ago, I knew about atonement. But my knowledge was incomplete and inadequate, and was based on preconceptions and misunderstandings. I thought the traditional view of atonement was the only acceptable one. But now, after a good deal of reading, I have come to a more complete understanding of the topic.

Update to what I know

I no longer see atonement as being needed because we enter the world fallen, condemned, and helpless. This idea is not found in the Genesis account of creation and is not in any way inspiring. But what is found there is an uplifting account of our origins as God's loved, trusted, and empowered children—a truly inspiring conception.

Judging from what Jesus taught, I believe that he embraced this type of positive view about human nature. What I gather from reading the Gospels is that Jesus saw atonement not as a need of the *wretched*, but as an opportunity for the *blessed*. Thus true atonement is rooted not in fear and shame, but in God-given confidence and healthy pride.

I still might think of Jesus as a savior, but in the sense that following him—implementing his principles in my life—can save me from believing that I am estranged from my heavenly Father. It can save me from self-destructive impulses. And it can save me from seeing myself as unworthy, corrupt, and incapable—a self conception that makes abundant living impossible. The purpose of Jesus' mission, as I now see it, was not to rescue the helpless, but to enlighten and motivate the capable. And I think that it is worthwhile to take his ideas seriously.

Course change

After doing considerable research, I have decided to let go of the conventional church view of atonement and instead to follow Jesus. Although he understood the need to narrow the divine-human gap created by sin, he never said that it could happen only by supernatural means. He stressed that each individual has the remarkable natural capability to be motivated by higher instincts and to turn away from sinfulness.

Jesus saw that atonement was useful not as a means of avoiding God's wrath, but as a means of drawing closer to God and fully experiencing His love, compassion, and mercy. I think what he taught makes sense. And I think I can benefit more from embracing his idea and believing in my capacity for righteous living than I can from believing in a church doctrine.

So the traditional view—that God will not allow me to draw close to Him except through a supernatural act of punishment that I had nothing to do with—is no longer serviceable. My Christian faith no longer depends on atonement being a particular type of *event.* It depends on Jesus being a particular type of *individual:* someone who believed that the process of inward transformation, brought about by heartfelt repentance, could help people draw closer to God. Thus atonement is no longer something that I simply acknowledge. Instead, it is a dynamic process in which I can *participate*. What an inspiring and challenging perspective!

Notes

[1] "Atonement." *The Free Dictionary*,
https://www.thefreedictionary.com/atonement
[2] "Atonement." *Encyclopaedia Britannica*,
https://www.britannica.com/topic/atonement-religion
[3] Abdul-Malik, Johari. "Atonement in Judaism, Christianity, and Islam." National Public Radio, 2012,
https://www.npr.org/2012/09/20/161486339/atonement-in-judaism-christianity-and-islam
[4] Romans 3:23
[5] Romans 6:23
[6] "Original Sin," *The Catholic Encyclopedia*. New Advent,
http://www.newadvent.org/cathen/11312a.htm
[7] Nathan, Peter. "The Original View of Original Sin." Vision, 2003, https://www.vision.org/the-original-view-of-original-sin-1140
[8] Romans 5:6
[9] Wallace, J. Warner. "What Does Christianity Say About the Nature of Humans? Five Honest Realities." Cold-Case Christianity, 2014,
https://coldcasechristianity.com/writings/what-does-christianity-say-about-the-nature-of-humans/
[10] Genesis 1:27, Genesis 2:15
[11] Mark 7:21-23
[12] Mark 10:15
[13] Matthew 5:14
[14] Luke 15:7

[15] Dollar, Jason. "Sinners in the Hands of an Angry God: Updated to Modern English." Glory Focus, 2015, https://gloryfocus.com/2015/03/12/sinners-in-the-hands-of-an-angry-god-updated-to-modern-english/

[16] Nahum 1:2

[17] Leviticus 10:1-2

[18] Genesis 19:24-25

[19] Genesis 6:7

[20] Arlandson, James M. "The Wrath of God in the Old Testament: 'The Law Brings Wrath.'" Bible.org, 2014, https://bible.org/article/wrath-god-old-testament-law-brings-wrath

[21] Romans 2:8

[22] Smith, Colin. "Six Things You Need to Know About God's Wrath." Unlocking the Bible, 2017, https://unlockingthebible.org/2017/05/six-things-you-need-to-know-about-gods-wrath/

[23] Luke 12:32

[24] Luke 15:11-32

[25] Psalm 23.1

[26] Fosdick, Harry Emerson. *The Man From Nazareth.* New York: Harper & Brothers, 1949.

[27] Matthew 7:19

[28] Matthew 7:2

[29] Genesis 19:26

[30] Ephesians 2:8-9

[31] "Article XX: Of Good Works." *The Augsburg Confession.* Project Wittenberg, http://www.iclnet.org/pub/resources/text/wittenberg/concord/web/augs-020.html

[32] *1689 Baptist Confession of Faith,* "Chapter 9." Association of Reformed Baptist Churches in America, http://www.arbca.com/1689-chapter9

[33] Graham, Jack. "4 Steps to Breaking Free from the Chains that Bind You." PowerPoint with Jack Graham, 2016, https://resources.jackgraham.org/resource-library/articles/4-steps-to-breaking-free-from-the-chains-that-bind-you

[34] Robinson, B. A. "Salvation: According to Paul." Religious Tolerance, 2002, https://www.religioustolerance.org/chr_savj3.htm

[35] Galatians 3:23-24

[36] "New Testament Books in Chronological Order." Grace Fellowship Church, 2019, https://www.gfcto.com/articles/bible-books/the-nt-chronologically

[37] Matthew 7:13-14

[38] Luke 6:35

[39] Matthew 7:4-5

[40] Luke 10:30-37

[41] Matthew 18:22

[42] Romans 10:9

[43] Matthew 3:2

[44] Peters, Ted. "Models of Atonement." Pacific Lutheran Theological Seminary, 2005, https://www.plts.edu/faculty-staff/documents/ite_models_atonement.pdf

[45] Matthew 5:3

[46] Matthew 5:20

[47] Matthew 7:21

[48] John 14:6

[49] Hick, John. Cited in Bishop, James, "Why There's Doubt on the Jesus' 'I am' Statements in the Gospel of John." Bishop's Encyclopedia of Religion, Society and Philosophy, 2018, https://jamesbishopblog.com/2018/06/06/why-theres-doubt-on-the-jesus-i-am-statements-in-the-gospel-of-john/

[50] Schuller, Robert H. "Introduction to John." *Possibility Thinkers Bible*. Nashville: Thomas Nelson Publishers, 1984.
[51] Mark 10:45
[52] John 10:11
[53] Luke 6:37

4. Trinity

Introduction

The word "trinity" can be used to refer to any group of three things or people; but it's rarely used to describe anything but God. Today, among mainstream religions, "the Trinity" is a Christian doctrine that envisions God as unified and yet triune, or having three natures. Neither Judaism nor Islam subscribe to the notion of a triune God. Hinduism recognizes multiple gods, but not in any way that aligns with the Christian concept.

The idea of the Trinity has played a central role in the Christian faith for centuries. And it has found its way into creeds, hymns, liturgies, and statements of faith.

But the Trinity is difficult to grasp and difficult to explain, as you can gather from this attempt by Gregory of Nyssa, a fourth century bishop:

> "The Son is glorified by the Spirit; the Father is glorified by the Son; again the Son has His glory from the Father; and the Only-begotten thus becomes the glory of the Spirit...In like manner,

again, Faith completes the circle, and glorifies
the Son by means of the Spirit, and the Father by
means of the Son."[1]

Others have tried to clarify the triune nature of God
using metaphors, geometric figures, and even creative
math. Here's how one writer effortlessly takes away the
mystery of the Trinity:

"Divinity is a quality; therefore, it should be
multiplied qualitatively like this: $1 \times 1 \times 1 =$
1...Persons are a quantity; therefore, they are
added quantitatively like this: $1 + 1 + 1 = 3$."[2]

Despite the fact that it cannot be fully comprehended,
the Trinity is still widely believed to be the only correct
way of imagining God. In fact, some think that its mysterious and unexplainable nature proves that it isn't a
human conception, but instead "presupposes a Divine revelation."[3]

Conventional view

The conventional Christian view is that the Bible describes God as existing in three persons: Father, Son (Jesus
Christ), and Holy Spirit, each being fully God and yet
constituting one God. The three persons are coequal, co-
eternal, and of the same substance. This view of the trinity
idea is unique to Christianity and forms its foundation.

I began researching the elements of this view to see
how they originated and how they developed. I wanted to
see whether each idea is actually critical to my Christian
faith, and why.

In this chapter, I'll talk about some of the fascinating
and eye opening facts and opinions I've uncovered about
the Trinity doctrine, and explain how they have shaped my
view of the concept.

Is the concept of trinity found in the Bible?

According to the HarperCollins Bible Dictionary, the word "Trinity"

> "... does not occur in the Bible." It was "...formulated in the post-biblical period, although the early stages of its development can be seen in the [New Testament]. Attempts to trace the origins still earlier (to the Old Testament literature) cannot be supported by historical-critical scholarship..."[4]

Nevertheless, many Christians believe that hints of a divine trinity are found in the Bible, and that the concept has been central to Christianity since its beginnings—or perhaps long before its beginnings:

> Then God said, "Let us make humankind in our image, according to our likeness..."[5]

Some insist that this passage from the first chapter of Genesis, because it represents God referring to Himself with "us" and "our," supports the notion of a triune God. But the plural pronouns are more likely the "royal us" and "royal our," used by the writer of Genesis to denote God's majesty.

Others put personal pronouns aside, choosing instead to find the Trinity implied in sentence structure:

> The Lord bless you and keep you; the Lord make his face to shine upon you, and be gracious to you; the Lord lift up his countenance upon you, and give you peace.[6]

Some, with inexplicable confidence, assert that this blessing in the book of Numbers, by using God's name three times, demonstrates "a preview of the Trinity."[7]

But for language that seems more explicit, people usually look to the New Testament, and in particular to this account in Matthew:

> And when Jesus had been baptized, just as he came up from the water, suddenly the heavens were opened to him and he saw the Spirit of God descending like a dove and alighting on him. And a voice from heaven said, "This is my Son, the Beloved, with whom I am well pleased."[8]

Many Christians also will cite other verses in the New Testament, written by Paul, as proof that the Trinity is found in the Bible. For example:

> I appeal to you, brothers and sisters, by our Lord Jesus Christ and by the love of the Spirit, to join me in earnest prayer to God on my behalf.[9]

> The grace of the Lord Jesus Christ, the love of God, and the communion of the Holy Spirit be with all of you.[10]

I thought that these verses supported the idea that the Trinity is a biblical concept—until I become aware of three things.

First, the capitalization of "Son" and "Spirit" implies that they are proper names. But that represents an editorial decision by translators. The original Greek manuscripts were written in all capital letters called uncials.[11]

Second, the word "the" before "holy spirit" is typically not found in the Greek texts. The use of the definite article represents an attempt by translators to harmonize the original texts with the Trinity doctrine. Consider this example from Mark:

> "I have baptized you with water; but he will baptize you with the Holy Spirit."[12]

The word "the" is not found in the original Greek, but has been added by translators. You can see this for yourself by consulting an online "interlinear Bible," such as the one at scripture4all.org.[13]

And third, when Father, son, and holy spirit are mentioned, they are never designated as divine persons within a unified godhead. All that is asserted is that the three exist and are important in some way.

So at most, we could say that the foundations for the idea of a triune God are found in the New Testament. But we have to look forward more than a hundred years to find the first clear articulation of the trinity concept. It was offered by Tertullian, a lawyer by training, around the turn of the third century. He was the first to use the terms *trinitas* ("trinity") and *persona* ("persons") in describing the nature of God.[14]

But it wasn't until the fourth century that the Trinity doctrine was established and declared to be the official view of the church. Two councils of bishops were instrumental in the development of the doctrine.

The Council of Nicaea was convened in 325 to decide on the exact nature of the son of God so the people of the Roman Empire would know what they were expected to believe. In the end, it was decreed that Christ was co-eternal with the Father and of the same "substance."[15]

At that point, no decision was reached about the nature of holy spirit. That didn't come until the Council of Constantinople met 56 years later. At that meeting, holy spirit was determined to be "...the Lord, the Giver of Life, Who proceeds from the Father..."[16] Then the Trinity doctrine was complete.

What did Jesus think?

Jesus was familiar with Scripture (our Old Testament), so he surely knew of the passages that could conceivably be hints at a triune God. But he apparently didn't find them compelling because he didn't use them in his teachings. He never mentioned the word "trinity" or spoke about God having a three-person nature.

Nevertheless, many point to this statement by Jesus, recorded in Matthew, as proof that he embraced the Trinity concept:

> "Go therefore and make disciples of all nations, baptizing them in the name of the Father and of the Son and of the Holy Spirit, and teaching them to obey everything that I have commanded you..."[17]

But merely mentioning son and holy spirit along with God the Father doesn't imply that Jesus must have thought of them as divine persons who are coequal to the Father. We can't say with confidence that he was putting forth the idea of a triune God. (It's also worth noting that he said, "that I have commanded you," not "that the son has commanded you.")

Jesus spent a good deal of time telling people what he thought was important: moral character, inward purity, humility, helpfulness, faith. If he had thought the idea of a triune God to be important, it seems like he would have taught it vigorously and in clear terms so average people could understand it. If seeing God as three persons was essential for abundant living, Jesus certainly would have made people aware of it.

Conclusion

The idea of a triune God is not explicitly presented by the Bible's writers. Although there are references to Father, son, and holy spirit (with capitalization added later by translators), we can't reasonably infer that the writers were trying to say that son and holy spirit were divine persons who were coequal to and coeternal with God the Father.

Early post-biblical Christian advocates put forth the concept of Trinity as we know it. But it wasn't until the Council of Constantinople, some fourteen generations after Jesus walked the earth, that church leaders declared "God in three persons" to be the only acceptable way of conceptualizing the deity.

If Jesus had thought that the apparent allusions to a triune God in Scripture had any significance, he certainly would have incorporated them into his teachings. If he had thought that believing in a trinity of divine persons was necessary for spiritual growth and salvation, he, being compassionate and loving, would have shared that with others.

Is the trinity concept unique to the Christian faith?

Until a few years ago, I thought that the idea of a triune God was one thing that set Christianity apart from other religions. And today, that is the case. No other major religion conceptualizes God as a holy trinity.

C. S. Lewis certainly thought that the trinity concept was unique to the Christian faith. He said that the most important difference between Christianity and all other religions is that

> "...in Christianity God is not a static thing—not even a person—but a dynamic, pulsating activity, a life, almost a kind of drama. Almost, if you will not think me irreverent, a kind of dance. The union between the Father and the Son is such a live concrete thing that this union itself is also a Person."[18]

But after a little research, I discovered that the trinity notion didn't originate when the Christian faith got started. It was central to many ancient religions.

For example, according to historian Arthur Weigall:

> "The ancient Egyptians...usually arranged their gods or goddesses in trinities: there was the trinity of Osiris, Isis, and Horus, the trinity of Amen, Mut, and Khonsu, the trinity of Khnum, Satis, and Anukis, and so forth..."[19]

Furthermore, the Sumarians had Anu, Enlil, and Ea, who controlled sky, earth, and water, respectively. And the Babylonians had Ishtar, Namakh (mother), and Marduk (son).[20]

So triple deities appeared in many cultures. Some were triadic (three entities interrelated in some way); some were triune (a being with three aspects or manifestations); and some were tripartite (having three body parts —heads, for example—where there would normally be one).[21]

Generally speaking, the number *3* seemed to hold a fascination for ancient civilizations. Even Aristotle himself praised it as being something special:

> "...the world and all that is in it is determined by the number three, since beginning and middle and end give the number of an 'all,' and the number they give is the triad."[22]

More recently, psychologist Carl Jung observed that the

> "...grouping in triads is something like an archetype of the history of religion on which the threefold Christian Trinity may well be modeled. Yet the Trinity is not an example of a triad, but of a tri-unity, a three-oneness...that is fundamentally different from the triad corresponding to a 'tri-theism.'"[23]

Others, of course, have not accepted the idea that belief in a divine trinity is different from tri-theism. Thomas Jefferson, notably, held Jesus in high esteem but rejected the Trinity doctrine, as evidenced in this 1821 letter:

> "When we shall have done away the incomprehensible jargon of the Trinitarian arithmetic...; when we shall have knocked down the artificial scaffolding, reared to mask from view the simple structure of Jesus...and got back to the pure and simple doctrines he inculcated, we shall then be truly and worthily his disciples..."[24]

Nevertheless, "God in three persons" is widely believed by Christians to be a monotheistic concept.

What did Jesus think?

I always thought that Jesus lived in an out-of-the-way and sparsely populated region. But the land of Judah (known today as Palestine) in Jesus' day was home to half a million people or more. It was a diverse and cosmopolitan area, and more urban than one might think.[25]

It was also a vibrant hub of commerce because of its unique location in the eastern Mediterranean region. Jerusalem was a busy trading area, made possible by its central position "...combined with favourable sea communications through the harbours of Ascalon, Jaffa, Gaza, and Ptolemais."[26] And as one historian noted, Galilee, where Jesus spent most of his time during his ministry, was "covered with roads to everywhere."[27]

With so many people passing through from other places, it's almost certain that Jesus learned about many non-Jewish cultures. So he likely knew about religions that venerated triads or trinities of some kind. But they apparently didn't capture his imagination. He never said anything about "persons" when talking about God. In the faith he had, and encouraged others to have, the trinity idea as we know it played no role.

Jesus didn't teach people to envision God as existing in three persons. If that notion had been essential to their spiritual wellbeing and to experiencing God's grace, it seems like he would have emphasized it over and over again. But Jesus kept it simple and talked about God in ways that anyone could easily comprehend: father, shepherd, friend.

So although the trinity idea might be unique to Christianity (since the year 381), it was not a feature of Jesus' unique faith that he lived and taught.

Conclusion

The trinity concept did not originate with Christianity. Many ancient faiths were built around three co-acting deities or gods with three aspects or natures. Early cultures in all parts of the world found the number *3* to have profound significance, and incorporated it into their religions.

But since the fourth century, Christianity has been the only major religion to embrace the idea that three persons constitute God. At the Council of Constantinople, bishops decided *for all time* what Christians must believe about the nature of God. Why so many Christians grant those clergymen such power and authority is unclear.

Jesus most likely knew about other religions that incorporated some kind of triple deity. But he evidently did not find the concept appealing or useful in any practical way. He didn't build his faith on the "three persons" idea. He didn't seem concerned about the theoretical *structure* of God. But he was concerned with something more practical: the *process* of God—the ways in which He can have an ongoing influence on people who desire to grow spiritually. And he tried to motivate people to make themselves receptive to that influence through repentance, service, and unshakable faith.

Is Jesus a member of a holy trinity?

The traditional view of trinity has Jesus as one of three God-persons, coequal to and coeternal with the Father and holy spirit. But how did that idea originate?

Miracles

I imagine that many people would bring up the miracles attributed to Jesus as proof of his divine nature. But I learned that, at the time, miracles were not considered the sole province of deities. *New World Encyclopedia* says:

> "Miracle workers were common in the ancient world. In fact, miracle workers were so common that miracles were not necessarily considered to be an authoritative sign of divine power..."[28]

As Harry Emerson Fosdick pointed out, in the time of Jesus "no organized knowledge of natural laws limited credulity; miracles...were expected and counted on..."[29]

And it's important to remember that Jesus said this:

> "...For truly I tell you, if you have faith the size of a mustard seed, you will say to this mountain, 'Move from here to there,' and it will move; and nothing will be impossible for you."[30]

What a fascinating statement! Jesus clearly thought that marvelous acts were within reach of any individual who had adequate faith.

So reports of wonderworks by Jesus are not compelling evidence that he was one of three God-persons in a holy trinity.

Jesus' disciples

The people who knew Jesus best—his disciples—saw in him qualities that they believed were God's qualities: mercy, love, compassion. And they even used two honor-ifics—messiah and son of God—to describe him:

> [Jesus asked,] "But who do you say that I am?" Simon Peter answered, "You are the Messiah, the Son of the living God."...Then [Jesus] sternly ordered the disciples not to tell anyone that he was the Messiah.[31]

I always thought that by allowing people to call him "messiah," Jesus was admitting that he was a God in human form. But I learned that the messiah hoped for by the Jewish people was not a divine figure. He was a man (warrior? priest? king?) who would restore Israel to great-ness and usher in a period of peace and prosperity. Theologian N. T. Wright says:

> "'Messiah,' or 'Christ,' does not mean 'the/a divine one.' It is very misleading to use the words as shorthands for the divine name or being of Jesus."[32]

Furthermore, "son of God" is not the same as "God the Son." Accepting the title "son of God" doesn't imply that Jesus was asserting that he was a member of a three-part godhead. (It's also worth noting that throughout human history, many have been called son of God, son of Heaven, or something similar.)[33]

The first Christians

What about the first Christians? Did they think that Jesus was a God-person? According to the written records, they thought of him as a unique and transcendent figure. But they did not assign divine status to him.

Paul wrote some of the earliest works that are included in the New Testament. Whether he thought of Jesus as being from the divine realm is debatable. But even if he did, it doesn't imply that he thought that Jesus was a divine person within a trinity. Consider the greeting in Paul's letter to the Philippians:

> Grace to you and peace from God our Father and the Lord Jesus Christ.[34]

All of the letters authored or coauthored by Paul include a similar greeting. What's conspicuously absent is any mention of holy spirit. So if he was trying to say that Jesus was a member of a triune God, he did a poor job of it in his greetings—and not just once, but more than a dozen times.

Other early Christians frequently spoke of Jesus as the "servant" of God. If they had thought that Jesus was co-eternal with and coequal to the Father, they certainly wouldn't have spoken of him as a subordinate.

Only in the Gospel of John is Jesus represented as making several statements that affirm a divine nature. But scholars generally do not consider such statements to be historically accurate.[35] Nevertheless, some Christians will cite this verse as proof that Jesus said he was God:

> "...Whoever has seen me has seen the Father..."[36]

But this isn't an unambiguous statement about Jesus being God. It doesn't imply that there aren't other ways to see the Father. Did not the traveler who was attacked in Jesus' parable of the Good Samaritan see the Father in the compassion and care of the man who stopped to help?

The author of John also has Jesus making this statement:

> "The Father and I are one."[37]

Even if this saying is authentic, there's no reason to think that Jesus was asserting that he, and only he, was one with the Father. His teachings are consistent with the idea that we all can be, or at least aspire to be, one with the Father.

What did Jesus think?

If Jesus believed that God existed in three persons, with himself as one of the divine persons, he could have expressed that idea at any time.

For example, instead of saying this:

> "You shall love the Lord your God with all your heart..."[38]

he could have said this:

> "You shall love the Lord your Father, and me, and holy spirit with all your heart..."

In fact, any time Jesus referred to God, he had the chance to make it crystal clear that he was "God the Son" and a member of a holy trinity. But he never did.

We do, however, find a number of statements indicating that Jesus did not think of himself as a God-person:

> ..."Why do you call me good? No one is good but God alone."[39]

> "...the Father is greater than I."[40]

Jesus clearly acknowledged the divine within himself—but also within every person. And he encouraged everyone to embrace that reality and believe it without reservation.

Conclusion

According to the written records, neither the disciples nor the first Christians thought of Jesus as a divine member of a trinity. Some did think of him as "messiah," and some called him "son of God." But those titles don't imply that they thought of Jesus as one of three God-persons.

It wasn't until the Council of Nicaea, in 325, that Jesus was declared to be of the "same substance" as God, co-equal to and coeternal with Him. (This raises some obvious questions: How could a group of clergymen have any idea what the "substance" of God is? And how could they possibly know whether all of the divine persons were precisely coequal and coeternal?)

Jesus accepted being called "son of God" and also "messiah." But he didn't say anything that definitively indicates that he saw himself as one of three members of a holy trinity. He did, however, realize that his relationship with God impressed those around him as remarkable. But Jesus made it clear that they, too, could have such a relationship. What is "follow me"[41] if not an invitation to "live as I live"?

Is God's nature best described in terms of persons?

The Catholic Encyclopedia describes the Trinity in a traditional way:

> "...in the unity of the Godhead there are Three Persons, the Father, the Son, and the Holy Spirit, these Three Persons being truly distinct one from another."[42]

We've all heard this, or something like it, so many times that it's almost impossible to think of the Trinity in any way other than as persons. But is that really the best way of describing God?

The nature of holy spirit

It's obviously easy to see Jesus as a person. And God the Father is often imagined with human characteristics, so it's possible to see Him as a person in some way. But did the Bible's writers think of holy spirit in a similar way? I did a little research and found that holy spirit is referred to in many ways that are inconsistent with the idea of personhood.

For example, we find that holy spirit is a gift;[43] it can be poured out;[44] it can renew us.[45] We can partake of it;[46] be filled with it;[47] and be baptized with it.[48]

Furthermore, holy spirit, unlike Father and son, is likened to a variety of nonhuman things: water;[49] fire;[50] wind;[51] a dove.[52]

More often than not, the Bible's writers didn't imagine holy spirit as a person. *New Catholic Encyclopedia* sums it up succinctly: "The majority of New Testament texts reveal God's spirit as something, not someone..."[53]

With all of this in mind, how is it that most Christians imagine holy spirit to be a person?

The primary reason seems to be that modern Bible translations are actually mistranslations, and reflect the biases of the translators.

Consider, for example, this verse from Luke:

> "...how much more will the heavenly Father give the Holy Spirit to those who ask him!"[54]

About this verse and others like it, one biblical researcher says that the Greek text

> "...quite clearly says 'a holy spirit'...However, the NIV (and nearly all other English translations) forces a trinitarian interpretation by translating it as 'the Holy Spirit' with the definite article and capitalization."[55]

Adding the definite article and capitalization gives the impression that holy spirit is a who, not a what, so as to conform to Trinity doctrine.

Moreover, in modern translations, holy spirit is almost always referred to with pronouns such as "he" and "who" rather than "it" and "which"—even though the Greek word *pneuma*, usually translated as spirit, also can mean breath or wind.[56]

So imagining God in terms of persons, with holy spirit being one of those persons, doesn't seem warranted based on what the New Testament authors actually said.

What did Jesus think?

Jesus never talked about knowing God as three persons. But he did talk about knowing God in three distinct ways.

Jesus understood that we can know God *personally*. For example, we can sense God's:

> Care: "Our Father...give us this day our daily bread."[57]

> Constant presence: "...your Father knows what you need before you ask him."[58]

> Concern: "...not one [sparrow] will fall to the ground apart from your Father... So do not be afraid; you are of more value than many sparrows."[59]

We experience God personally when we pray, or meditate, or repent. And when it happens, it confirms that God is *within* us.

Jesus also understood that we can know God *interpersonally*, that is, through interactions with others. He encouraged people to elevate such interactions by acting selflessly to experience God's:

Mercy: "Our Father...forgive us our debts, as we also have forgiven our debtors."[60]

Generosity: "Give to everyone who begs from you, and do not refuse anyone who wants to borrow from you."[61]

Universal goodwill: "...Love your enemies and pray for those who persecute you, so that you may be children of your Father in heaven..."[62]

We experience God interpersonally when we help or are helped, when we encourage or are encouraged, when we show mercy or receive mercy. And when it happens, it confirms that God is *among* us.

Finally, Jesus understood that we can know God *impersonally*. We can become aware of things that we cannot possibly comprehend, such as God's:

Holiness: "Our Father...hallowed be your name."[63]

Omnipresence: "...Lord of heaven and earth..."[64]

Power: "...for God all things are possible."[65]

We experience God impersonally when we gaze at the stars, or imagine the moment of creation, or try to grasp the ideas of omnipotence and omniscience. And when it happens, it confirms that God is *beyond* us.

Jesus didn't espouse a trinity of divine persons. But he did recognize a trinity of experiences with the one God who is simultaneously within us, among us, and beyond us. He just never associated a unique person with each type of experience. He seemed to understand that God is relational in nature—an idea that fits with actual experience and requires no metaphysical speculation.

Conclusion

The traditional view of trinity was put forth in the fourth century, and has remained virtually unchanged to this day: three God-persons—Father, son, and holy spirit—constitute the deity. Despite the fact that it is incomprehensible, many believe that this is the best way to describe God.

But there is no clear biblical support for the trinity concept. Only in biased translations do we see evidence of a triune God. Only when the original Greek texts are manipulated to conform to Trinity doctrine is the idea of "God in three persons" evident in Scripture.

Jesus never said that he believed God could best be understood as three persons. But he did recognize that we can understand God in three distinct ways: personally, such as when we connect with Him by prayer; interpersonally, through encounters with others; and impersonally, through awareness of the infinite, incomprehensible Creator. This kind of trinity is not a theological construct, but a useful and practical awareness of God's diverse ways of revealing Himself to us, and in us, in everyday life.

Summary

A few years ago, I knew about the Trinity, of course. After all, I had sung the "Doxology" (the last line being "Praise Father, Son, and Holy Ghost") several thousand times. But I had no idea about how the idea came about or developed. So I decided to replace my ignorance with facts and critical evaluations. It was a gradual process, but now I have a much better grasp of the topic.

Update to what I know

I no longer accept the idea that the Trinity is a biblical concept. It's not presented in the Old Testament, taught by Jesus, or promoted by the earliest Christians who wrote the New Testament. Although Father, son, and holy spirit are mentioned a number of times (with capitalization added by translators), they are never identified as members of a holy trinity.

Considering what Jesus did and did not teach, I believe that he wasn't concerned with the structure of God. His focus was on God's *process*—the ways in which He interacts with us. And Jesus' teachings point to three types of encounters that we can have with God: personal, where we experience God within us; interpersonal, where we experience God among us; and impersonal, where we experience God beyond us.

I don't need to engage in philosophical speculation to grasp this type of trinity—I just need to live my life with an awareness of God's presence and an expectation of encounters with Him on different levels. I'm not sure that assigning "persons" to those experiences makes them more real or meaningful.

Course change

Based on what I now know, I've decided to abandon the traditional church view of trinity and instead to follow Jesus. Although he understood that God reveals Himself in diverse ways, he didn't encourage people to see God as triune. He never taught that God's nature could best be understood in terms of three divine persons.

Jesus' teaching show that he thought that God can best be understood in terms of three types of relationships: personal, when I experience His presence; interpersonal, when I experience His compassion; and impersonal, when

I experience His mystery. I think that this conception makes sense and fits with actual experience. And I think I can benefit more from actively seeking these experiences than from passively believing a doctrine that is incomprehensible.

So the traditional view—that I must see my interactions with God in terms of divine persons—is no longer viable. My Christian faith no longer depends on God having a particular *structure*. It depends on Jesus being a particular type of *individual:* someone who understood that God's process involves being simultaneously within us, among us, and beyond us, allowing us to know Him in three unique ways. Thus the trinity is no longer something that I observe from a distance. Instead, it is a dynamic process in which I can *participate*. What an uplifting and empowering perspective!

Notes

[1] Gregory of Nyssa. "On the Holy Spirit, Against the Followers of Macedonius." Bible Study Tools, https://www.biblestudytools.com/history/early-church-fathers/post-nicene/vol-5-gregory-of-nyssa/gregory-of-nyssa/holy-spirit-against-followers-of-macedonius.html

[2] Rochford, James M. "Defending the Trinity." Evidence Unseen, http://www.evidenceunseen.com/theology/christian-doctrine/defending-the-doctrine-of-the-trinity/

[3] "The Blessed Trinity." *The Catholic Encyclopedia*. New Advent, http://www.newadvent.org/cathen/15047a.htm

[4] Achtemeier, Paul J., ed. "Trinity." *The HarperCollins Bible Dictionary*. San Francisco: HarperOne, 1996.

[5] Genesis 1:26

[6] Numbers 6:24-26

[7] Sanders, Fred. "What Does the Old Testament say about the Trinity?" Zondervan Academic, 2017, https://zondervanacademic.com/blog/what-does-the-old-testament-say-about-the-trinity
[8] Matthew 3:16-17
[9] Romans 15:30
[10] 2 Corinthians 13:14
[11] Shaw, Benjamin. "Punctuating the Bible." 2011, http://gptsrabbi.blogspot.com/2011/10/punctuating-bible.html
[12] Mark 1:8
[13] *Greek Interlinear Bible (NT)*. Scripture4all Publishing, https://www.scripture4all.org/OnlineInterlinear/Greek_Index.htm
[14] Pearse, Roger. "Tertullian's Theology." Tertullian.org., http://www.tertullian.org/theology.htm
[15] "Trinity." Religion Facts, 2017, http://www.religionfacts.com/trinity
[16] "The Nicene-Constantinopolitan Creed," http://web.mit.edu/ocf/www/nicene_creed.html
[17] Matthew 28:19-20
[18] Lewis, C. S. *Mere Christianity*. Harper Collins, 1952. Digitized version page 85, https://www.dacc.edu/assets/pdfs/PCM/merechristianitylewis.pdf
[19] Weigall, Arthur. *Paganism in Our Christianity,* 1928, pp. 197-198. Cited at "How Ancient Trinitarian Gods Influenced Adoption of the Trinity." United Church of God, https://www.ucg.org/bible-study-tools/booklets/is-god-a-trinity/how-ancient-trinitarian-gods-influenced-adoption-of-the-trinity
[20] Pantovic, Nuit Natasa. "Trinity in World Religions." Times Internet Limited, 2013, https://www.speakingtree.in/blog/trinity-in-world-religions

[21] "Triple Deity." Enacademic, 2010,
https://enacademic.com/dic.nsf/enwiki/11533662
[22] Aristotle. *De Caelo (On the Heavens)*, Book I. Trans. J. L.
Stocks, http://classics.mit.edu/Aristotle/heavens.1.i.html
[23] Jung, Carl. "On the Psychology of the Concept of the
Trinity." (Lecture delivered in 1940). The Jung Center, 2013,
http://www.cgjungpage.org/learn/articles/analytical-
psychology/184-on-the-psychology-of-the-concept-of-the-
trinity
[24] "Jefferson's Religious Beliefs." Monticello.org.,
https://www.monticello.org/site/research-and-
collections/jeffersons-religious-beliefs
[25] Olsen, Ted. "The Life & Times of Jesus of Nazareth: Did You
Know?" Christianity Today,
https://www.christianitytoday.com/history/issues/issue-
59/life-times-of-jesus-of-nazareth-did-you-know.html
[26] Jeremias, Joachim. *Jerusalem in the Time of Jesus.*
Philadelphia, PA: Fortress Press, 3rd edition, 1962. Trans. F.
H. and C. H. Cave,
http://khazarzar.skeptik.net/books/jremias2.pdf
[27] Smith, George Adam, *Historical Geography of the Holy
Land.* New York: A. C. Armstrong & Son, 1901, page 425,
https://archive.org/details/historicalgeogra00smit_0/page/
424
[28] "Miracle." *New World Encyclopedia,*
https://www.newworldencyclopedia.org/entry/Miracle
[29] Fosdick, Harry Emerson. *The Man From Nazareth*. New
York: Harper & Brothers, 1949, page 55.
[30] Matthew 17:20
[31] Matthew 16: 15-16, 20
[32] N. T. Wright. "Jesus' Self-Understanding." NTWrightPage,
2002, http://ntwrightpage.com/2016/04/05/jesus-self-
understanding/

[33] "Son of God." New World Encyclopedia,
https://www.newworldencyclopedia.org/entry/Son_of_God
[34] Philippians 1:2
[35] Bishop, James, "Why There's Doubt on the Jesus' 'I am'
Statements in the Gospel of John." Bishop's Encyclopedia of
Religion, Society and Philosophy, 2018,
https://jamesbishopblog.com/2018/06/06/why-theres-
doubt-on-the-jesus-i-am-statements-in-the-gospel-of-john/
[36] John 14:9
[37] John 10:30
[38] Luke 10:27
[39] Luke 18:19
[40] John 14:28
[41] Matthew 4:19
[42] Joyce, George. "The Blessed Trinity." *The Catholic
Encyclopedia.* Vol. 15. New York: Robert Appleton
Company, 1912,
http://www.newadvent.org/cathen/15047a.htm
[43] Acts 10:45
[44] Acts 2:17
[45] Titus 3:5
[46] Hebrews 6:4
[47] Acts 2:4
[48] Matthew 3:11
[49] John 4:14
[50] Acts 2:3
[51] Acts 2:2
[52] Matthew 3:16
[53] "Spirit of God." *New Catholic Encyclopedia*, 2nd. edition,
2003, vol. 13, page 428,
https://cvdvn.files.wordpress.com/2018/05/new-catholic-
encyclopedia-vol-13.pdf
[54] Luke 11:13

[55] Davidson, Paul. "Poor and Misleading Translation in the New International Version (NIV)," https://isthatinthebible.wordpress.com/articles-and-resources/deliberate-mistranslation-in-the-new-international-version-niv/

[56] Schoenheit, John. "God's Gift of holy spirit—a 'He' or an 'It.'" Spirit & Truth Fellowship International, 2013, https://www.truthortradition.com/articles/gods-gift-of-holy-spirit-a-he-or-an-it

[57] Matthew 6:9, 11

[58] Matthew 6:8

[59] Matthew 10:29-31

[60] Matthew 6:9, 12

[61] Matthew 5:42

[62] Matthew 5:44-45

[63] Matthew 6:9-10

[64] Matthew 11:25

[65] Matthew 19:26

5. Resurrection

Introduction

Shakespeare's Hamlet imagines death to be "the undiscover'd country from whose bourn [realm] no traveler returns."[1] Hamlet apparently never attended an Easter sunrise service. If he had, he would have found out that many people throughout the world believe that one traveler—Jesus of Nazareth—did return, in some sense, from the "undiscover'd country." They believe that he was resurrected.

Most people understand "resurrection" to mean the return to life after death. The term doesn't necessarily imply immortality. After all, one conceivably could return to life for only a limited time. But it's unlikely that many people today think of resurrection without thinking of eternal life.

Christianity is not the only faith that incorporates the idea of resurrection. Islam, for example, teaches that at Doomsday all will die and then be raised, after which all will be judged. And Zoroastrianism "holds a belief in a final overthrow of Evil, a general resurrection, a Last Judgment, and the restoration of a cleansed world to the righteous."[2]

Although Christianity also teaches a general resurrection, at its core is the resurrection of one individual—Jesus. And his experience is thought by many to have been unique.

Like all other ideas in the faith, resurrection and its implications have been vigorously debated for centuries. And they most likely will continue to be debated as long as there are people calling themselves Christians.

Conventional view

The conventional Christian view of resurrection is that Jesus, a few days after his burial, arose from the grave with a restored body. Leaving the empty tomb behind, he went out and interacted with others over a forty-day period. Then he ascended to heaven, from which he will someday return, initiating the resurrection of all.

I began investigating these ideas to see how they came about and developed over the years. I wanted to see whether each element is actually indispensible in my Christian faith, and why.

In this chapter, I'll share some of the interesting and surprising facts I've come across, and explain how and why my discoveries have led to a change of opinion about resurrection.

Did the resurrection of Jesus actually occur?

Composer Lani Smith poses this question in his brilliant musical "Jubilation!":

> If Jesus hadn't risen / Then how do you explain
> the sudden change in his disciples? / In a very

> little while their despair had turned to joy / And
> they preached and healed with a power just like
> Jesus.[3]

This is a provocative question that can't be ignored. The disciples' teacher, their Master, was dead, executed as a heretic. And he hadn't accomplished what the messiah was supposed to accomplish. The bright future they had envisioned would not unfold. So they naturally were in a sad and hopeless state. But then there was a change. A fire was lit, and they began spreading the new faith with unsurpassed zeal and courage. The only reasonable reaction to this is: Wow!

It's undeniable that something dramatic happened to bring about the change. At the time, it was understood as resurrection. So resurrection did in fact occur. The important question is: What, exactly, is meant by "resurrection"?

To find out what it meant to the earliest Christians, we need to look at two types of experiences recorded in the New Testament: the empty tomb and Jesus' appearances. You might be surprised, as I was, to learn that the *appearances* were recorded first. We know this because scholars have been able to arrange the books of the New Testament in approximate chronological order, which is quite different from the arrangement we find in today's Bibles.[4]

The appearance accounts

The earliest known reference to the resurrection of Jesus was written by Paul of Tarsus in his first letter to the Christians in Corinth around the year 55 (twenty years or so after Jesus' execution):

> For I handed on to you as of first importance
> what I in turn had received: that Christ died for

> our sins in accordance with the scriptures, and
> that he was buried, and that he was raised on
> the third day in accordance with the scrip-
> tures, and that he appeared to Cephas, then to
> the twelve. Then he appeared to more than five
> hundred brothers and sisters at one time...Then
> he appeared to James, then to all the apos-
> tles. Last of all, as to one untimely born, he
> appeared also to me.[5]

It's important to note Paul's repeated use of the word
"appeared." This indicates something different from a nor-
mal encounter with an individual. For example, if my
neighbor Sam comes to my house, I wouldn't later tell my
friends that Sam *appeared* to me. But I might say that if I
had a vision of Sam or a dream about him.

Paul didn't believe in resurrection of the flesh. The
"risen" Christ to him was a spiritual presence. And in the
same letter to the Corinthians, Paul makes his position
clear about the nature of the resurrected "body":

> ...For the trumpet will sound, and the dead will
> be raised imperishable, and we will be changed.
> For this perishable body must put on imperish-
> ability, and this mortal body must put on im-
> mortality.[6]

So the earliest testimony to the continued existence of
Jesus comes from one who believed that Jesus was resurrected, but did not believe in reanimation of a lifeless
physical body.[7] It would be at least fifteen years before
resurrection stories involving a restored body started to
circulate.

The empty tomb accounts

In Mark, the earliest Gospel (written around the year 70), we don't find any record of appearances by Jesus. And one researcher notes that there is "...strong textual evidence that the *first generation of Jesus followers* were perfectly fine with a Gospel account that recounted *no appearances of Jesus.*" (Verses 9–20 of the final chapter of Mark, which mention appearances, are considered by most scholars not to be part of the original text.)[8]

But the first Gospel writer does mention an empty tomb.[9] And over the next thirty years, Matthew, Luke, and John produced their Gospels and also included accounts of an empty tomb. But there are a number of irreconcilable differences among the stories, such as the time of day, the people who visited the tomb, and what happened afterward.[10]

Many Christians probably assume that the empty tomb stories *created* belief in Jesus' resurrection. But as New Testament scholar Bart Ehrman observes, an empty tomb wouldn't be convincing proof:

> "If you put somebody in a tomb and three days later you go back and the body's not in the tomb, your first thought isn't, 'Oh, he's been exalted to heaven and made the son of God.' Your first thought is, 'Somebody stole the body.' Or, 'Somebody moved the body.' Or, 'Hey, I'm at the wrong tomb'...In the New Testament it's striking that... the empty tomb leads to confusion but it doesn't lead to belief. What leads to belief is that some of the followers of Jesus have visions of him afterward."[11]

So the appearances were the first encounters with the risen Jesus to be recorded. The "body" of Jesus was viewed as ethereal and suitable for the immortal realm. As time went by, and the story was retold many times, the empty tomb element was introduced and Jesus started taking on a more *physical* nature: he walked, ate food, touched people. So some of the faithful at the time obviously believed that the decaying corpse of Jesus in the grave was the one restored during his resurrection. (But not *fully* restored, apparently. One account in John[12] mentions nail scars on Jesus' hands.)

What did Jesus think?

According to the Gospel accounts, Jesus had no doubt that he would experience resurrection. But he didn't go into details about how or why it would occur. Nor did he express an opinion about what type of "body" he would have.

Jesus believed that life is eternal, and that death merely serves as a transition between the mortal and immortal worlds. And he apparently saw it as a relatively quick transition:

> ..."The Son of Man must...be killed, and on the
> third day be raised."[13]

Jesus didn't offer arguments for immortality. He apparently took it for granted. But he introduced his followers to "a quality of life that incalculably elevated for them the significance of living."[14] Fellowship with God became a vital experience and left no doubt that life continued after our time in this world.

Conclusion

In the days following Jesus' death, his disciples felt his continued presence and influence intensely. And they interpreted their experiences in the only way that made sense to them: Jesus had been resurrected. This awareness motivated them to risk everything to spread the new faith that focused on Jesus and eternal life.

The earliest Christians thought in terms of *bodily* resurrection because that is what they had been taught. But there was disagreement about what "body" meant. The first documented experiences with the post-Easter Jesus were *spiritual* encounters such as dreams and visions, implying that Jesus was believed to have a *non-physical* body. Only much later were accounts written that included an empty tomb and encounters with an increasingly substantial Jesus.

It seems clear that Jesus believed that he (and everyone else) would be resurrected. Thus death could be viewed as a transition, not a state. And this makes sense given Jesus' emphasis on God's kingdom. If we enter the kingdom here and now, why should we think that death would remove us from it for some period of time?

Did Jesus' experience make possible a general resurrection?

Many in the Christian community are probably convinced that Jesus had an experience after death that had not previously been imagined. But in fact, the faithful had heard about resurrection long before the Gospel accounts were written. The idea had been part of Jewish thought for centuries.

According to the *HarperCollins Bible Dictionary:*

> "The concept of resurrection is derived from Jewish apocalyptic literature. In earlier [Old Testament] writings there is no belief in life after death...When eventually this belief developed, it was in the form of resurrection of the dead, rather than the immortality of the soul..."[15]

I was able to find only a few hopeful statements about life after death in the Old Testament, including this well-known one in Isaiah:

> Your dead shall live, their corpses shall rise. O
> dwellers in the dust, awake and sing for joy! For
> your dew is a radiant dew, and the earth will
> give birth to those long dead.[16]

In the Old Testament, references to life after death are few. But in the New Testament there is an emphasis on eternal life. By the time of Jesus, resurrection was well established in Jewish thought. (It wasn't universally accepted, however. The Sadducees—a conservative religious/political group who relied only on the written law of Moses—rejected the idea of resurrection.)[17]

But how did the idea of resurrection develop? To find its beginnings, we need to go back many generations before Jesus.

The origins of resurrection

The ancient Hebrew cosmos had three tiers: a flat earth; heaven above; and Sheol, the abode of the departed, below the earth's surface. Sheol was a sad place where people still existed, but only as insubstantial beings. Existence after death was so pale that no hopes were associated with it. Originally, Yahweh was considered to have nothing to do with Sheol. But as people began to imagine his scope expanding, his influence over that realm became accepted. Sheol stopped being a meaningless place, and became a place where rewards and punishments are administered. It became morally meaningful. Thus came hope of restoration from it.

The expectation of a coming Messianic age focused attention on the question of individual destiny: Should the restored kingdom benefit only the lucky people alive when it is established? How could the Messianic reign on earth be ethically complete if those who sacrificed greatly remained in Sheol? The land of the dead was portrayed so negatively that the only meaningful hope was reembodiment and restoration *to the earth*. Therefore, future hope and physical resurrection were bound together long before Jesus was born.[18]

The early Christian view

Paul clearly believed that Jesus' resurrection made possible a general resurrection:

> But in fact Christ has been raised from the dead, the first fruits of those who have died...for as all die in Adam, so all will be made alive in Christ.[19]

> Therefore we have been buried with him by baptism into death, so that, just as Christ was raised from the dead by the glory of the Father, so we too might walk in newness of life.[20]

In his writings, Paul takes the old idea of a general resurrection and ties it to Jesus. He believes that Jesus' resurrection had to occur before others could experience it. But Paul doesn't say anything about Jesus *actively* bringing about the resurrection of others at a particular time. He just gives the opinion that we all will experience rebirth in the same way Jesus did—by being "raised" by God.

The HarperCollins Bible Dictionary sums up the early church's beliefs:

> "The post-Easter proclamation of Jesus' resurrection is to be seen in the context of Jewish apocalyptic hope. His resurrection is an act of God, who raised him from the dead as the "first fruits" in anticipation of the general resurrection

...The resurrection of the believers would follow
as a result of Christ's resurrection..."[21]

What did Jesus think?

Jesus was a Jew, and was well acquainted with Scripture (he quoted from it frequently). So he knew of the
concept of resurrection. And we're told in the Gospels that
he referred to it on several occasions.

But in the three Synoptic Gospels (Mark, Matthew, and
Luke), Jesus never says that the resurrection of others depends on him. He doesn't claim that *he* will be responsible
for "raising" people from death. In fact, he makes it clear
that he thinks that resurrection has been occurring for
quite a while without his involvement:

> "And the fact that the dead are raised Moses
> himself showed, in the story about the bush,
> where he speaks of the Lord as the God of
> Abraham, the God of Isaac, and the God of Jacob.
> Now he is God not of the dead, but of the living;
> for to him all of them are alive."[22]

Only in the Fourth Gospel is Jesus presented as making
inflated statements about his role in the resurrection of
others:

> "...the hour is coming when all who are in their
> graves will hear [the Son of Man's] voice and will
> come out..."[23]

> "This is indeed the will of my Father, that all who
> see the Son and believe in him may have eternal
> life; and I will raise them up on the last day."[24]

Here, Jesus is presented as taking center stage in the
process of resurrection. But John's Jesus is incompatible
with the Jesus we find in the three earlier Synoptic Gos-

pels. And scholars generally agree that John is best interpreted as a theological statement, not a reliable historical document.[25]

> "The picture John then presents us with is a view of the Jesus tradition which has been heavily coloured and influenced by John and his own situation."[26]

But even if these statements in John are authentic, they still don't imply that Jesus meant that his *resurrection* is what would make possible the resurrection of others.

If Jesus had taught that he was to be the active agent in a general resurrection—something the Jewish people had long hoped for—the earlier Gospel writers surely would have mentioned it. But it was only near the turn of the second century that the imaginative author of John portrayed Jesus in this way.

Conclusion

The idea of a general resurrection was central to Jewish faith long before Jesus' ministry. It was understood as an important part of God's justice: The faithful who had died certainly would be returned to the earth to take part in the restored kingdom. And bodies of some kind would be needed. The idea of existence without a body was unimaginable.

Paul, and later the Gospel writers, promoted the idea that a general resurrection would be made possible by Jesus' resurrection. But Paul didn't opine that Jesus would *actively* restore the dead to life. He said that he believed we would "walk in newness of life" *in the same way Christ did.*

Jesus never said anything about being what Paul would later call the "first fruits" of the dead. He didn't teach that his experience would "pave the way" for the resurrection of others. Even in the Gospel of John, Jesus never says that a general resurrection will be made possible by his resurrection. Jesus seemed to believe that resurrection was natural and inevitable—for himself and for others.

Will the resurrected Jesus someday return to earth?

Traditional Christianity holds that Jesus will someday return to earth, ushering in a new era of the kingdom of God. The idea has captured imaginations ever since Jesus uttered his final words: "...I am with you always, to the end of the age."[27]

Jesus' "second coming" has been so intriguing that many people throughout the Christian era have felt the need to predict when it will occur. Among them are Renaissance painter Sandro Botticelli, all-around genius Isaac Newton, Methodist Church founder John Wesley, and self-professed psychic Edgar Cayce. Their predictions, as is true with almost all predictions about future events, were wrong.

So it's still possible that Jesus will return. But exactly how, when, and why are matters that are open to debate.

The ascension

The first step in returning is obviously to leave. And this is how Luke describes Jesus' departure:

> Then [Jesus] led [the disciples] out as far as Bethany, and, lifting up his hands, he blessed them. While he was blessing them, he withdrew from them and was carried up into heaven.[28]

Luke seems to imply that Jesus' trip was short and quick. This is not surprising, given how people saw the world in biblical times. The prevailing view was that the earth was flat, and heaven was just a short distance above the surface. In that kind of world, and at that time in human development, it would be easy to think of Jesus' goodbye as an ascent to a place just above the clouds. Then his return would involve a relatively easy descent the short distance back to earth.

Paul and the early church

Paul clearly believed that Jesus would someday return:

> ...as all die in Adam, so all will be made alive in Christ. But each in his own order: Christ the first fruits, then at his coming those who belong to Christ.[29]

So Paul's idea seems to be that the resurrected Jesus will come at a particular moment, and then believers will be "made alive." But when will that moment be?

> For the Lord himself...will descend from heaven, and the dead in Christ will rise first. Then we who are alive, who are left, will be caught up in the clouds together with them to meet the Lord in the air; and so we will be with the Lord forever.[30]

Notice that Paul believes that "we who are alive" will participate. So he, like most at the time, believed that Jesus' return—and the establishment of a new earthly kingdom—would happen within his lifetime. The fact that it didn't happen created a great deal of confusion and anxiety for the early Christians. And they dealt with the problem by shifting their focus to resurrection and eternal life.

So in his letters, Paul expresses two opinions: First, the resurrected Jesus will return from heaven—but Paul doesn't say that he thinks Jesus will return *bodily* to the

surface of the earth. And second, the return will be followed by a general resurrection of those in the state of
death—but he doesn't say he thinks that Jesus will play an
active role in the process.

How will the general resurrection occur?

You might think that there would be agreement on how
Jesus will bring about the general resurrection. But there's
not. Here are the three dominant beliefs about what might
happen:

> "Amillenialists believe that Jesus will return to
> earth and at that time the resurrection of the
> dead will take place along with the establish-
> ment of the New Heaven and the New Earth.

> "Postmillennialists believe that there will be a
> 'millennial age'...characterized by Christianity
> becoming the dominant religion and the world
> turning towards God. At the end of this age,
> Christ will return and the resurrection of the
> dead will take place.

> "Finally, premillenialists hold that...when Christ
> returns to earth...there will be a millennial age in
> which Christ reigns on earth. At the end of this
> time...the resurrection of unbelievers will occur
> and the New Heaven and New Earth will be
> established."[31]

Such distinctions are interesting. But they seem pointless and really have nothing to do with spiritual growth or
fellowship with God. And they no doubt keep people out of
the faith who otherwise might find it irresistible.

What did Jesus think?

Jesus mentioned his belief in his imminent resurrection on several occasions. But he never talked about ascending to heaven in an observable way.

Concerning a return to earth, Jesus said very little. And most of what he said is figurative and symbolic. For example, Mark records Jesus as saying this:

> "But in those days, after that suffering, the sun will be darkened, and the moon will not give its light, and the stars will be falling from heaven, and the powers in the heavens will be shaken. Then they will see 'the Son of Man coming in clouds' with great power and glory. Then he will send out the angels, and gather his elect from the four winds, from the ends of the earth to the ends of heaven."[32]

Jesus typically spoke to people in plain language, using images that they understood: farmers, widows, coins, seeds, sheep. But here we see the bizarre imagery of apocalyptic language, which is quite different from conventional language.

> "Apocalyptic literature is like a dream world; it's an image here and a saying there and a voice here. It's strange literature. It deals with end times; it has strange images; it's about God intervening in history; it's not history. It's not sequential; it doesn't claim to tell the whole story."[33]

We no longer use apocalyptic language, so it's hard to grasp exactly what Jesus meant with his provocative statement. And I haven't found a consensus about what the statement might imply. But even if we take the words literally, "coming in clouds" wouldn't necessarily imply the bodily return of Jesus to the surface of the earth that some believers envision.

We also need to question the timing of his return:

> "Truly I tell you, there are some standing here who will not taste death before they see the Son of Man coming in his kingdom."[34]

The fact that Jesus didn't return within a few years is a problem—but only if his "coming in his kingdom" is seen as a literal event. If he meant it as a spiritual event, then his "return" could occur at any time in a receptive individual.

Conclusion

Paul, writing twenty or more years after Jesus' execution, gave his opinion that Jesus would return *soon*, at which time a general resurrection would commence. So Paul believed that death was a *state* from which we needed to be delivered—the traditional point of view. And he thought that Jesus' resurrection made that delivery possible.

But Paul didn't say that he believed that Jesus would return *bodily* to the surface of the earth. Because Paul didn't believe in resurrection of the flesh, he had in mind a *spiritual* return. Such a return would take place as all people in all nations embraced the Christ spirit within them.

Jesus accepted the idea that all would experience resurrection. But the evidence that he believed *he* would return to earth to bring it about is scant. His statements about "coming" again are either figurative or lacking in specifics. And the exact nature of his return is unclear, although it seems to me that he thought it would be spiritual.

Is the traditional view of resurrection the most beneficial one?

To Jesus' followers, his death changed everything at first. Then a short time later, it changed little. They realized that they still felt his presence, his influence, his guidance as strongly as ever. Then they came to understand with certainty that death is merely a transition. And the only way they had of interpreting their experience was with the inherited idea of "rising from death."

Paul believed in spiritual, not bodily, resurrection. And yet in describing his encounter with the resurrected Jesus, he referred to Jesus' being "raised."[35] So "...apparently that metaphor had already become a central part of the vocabulary Jesus followers used in describing their experiences."[36]

The "rising from death" interpretation is still central in the faith of many Christians. And it is found in creeds, in liturgies, and even in a classic hymn:

> Up from the grave He arose / With a mighty
> triumph o'er His foes,[37]

But is this view really the best way of thinking about resurrection? Is it the most useful way of grasping its essence in today's world?

Symbolic resurrection

Some have rejected the traditional view of resurrection and have decided that it is best seen in symbolic terms. Here's how one academic puts it:

> "...we can reach the lowest points of our lives, of going deep into a place that feels like death, and then find our way out again—that's the story the Resurrection now tells me."[38]

Such a view might be helpful in some ways, but it minimizes the disciples' profound experiences following the death of Jesus. It suggests that they merely put a positive spin on a depressing situation and came to believe in their capacity to overcome their sadness. But it's hard to imagine that interpreting resurrection symbolically would have created the remarkable desire in Jesus' followers to vigorously spread the new faith.

Old and new interpretations

It's interesting that we've left behind many biblical-era interpretations. For example, we no longer view malicious demons as being the cause of afflictions. We no longer think of women as being inferior to men. We no longer see the universe as having been assembled in just a few days.

But when it comes to resurrection, many Christians cling to the ancient Jewish view of resurrection as "rising from death." After all, it's familiar and comfortable. But that doesn't mean that we must forever use it.

The experiences we have today in trying to grasp eternal life are the same as those of people long ago. But we categorize our experiences differently than they did. So we can believe in immortality without accepting the framework in which it was originally presented. We can apply a fresh perspective if it makes resurrection more vital and useful in our lives.

So with this in mind, why not phrase resurrection in another way that might be more helpful? For example, we could think of it as:

"leaving mortality behind."

"transitioning to the next phase of life."

"becoming unfettered by time and space."

The problem with the traditional view is that it sees death as a *state* from which we need to be delivered. But the disciples believed that they encountered the resurrected Jesus just *days* after his burial. So if death is a state, it is certainly a brief one.

What did Jesus think?

Jesus, being a Jew, inherited the traditional view of resurrection as "rising from death." But I think he tried to break free from its constraints by adding a *practical* dimension.

In my view, Jesus did a remarkable thing: he shifted the starting point of resurrection. Rebirth was something to experience *here and now, again and again during our earthly lives*, as well as beyond.

Jesus encouraged people to leave the lifeless world of sinfulness and rise to a higher level, which he called abundant living. He kept challenging people to ascend *continually* to a new quality of life. Consider these sayings:

> Jesus said to [Peter], "[Forgive] not seven times, but, I tell you, seventy-seven times."[39] In other words, "rise above pettiness and bitterness."

> ..."Truly I tell you, unless you change and become like children, you will never enter the kingdom of heaven."[40] In other words, "rise above arrogance and unhealthy pride."

> ..."if you have faith and do not doubt...even if you say to this mountain, 'Be lifted up and thrown into the sea,' it will be done."[41] In other words, "rise above weakness and timidity."

It's obvious that Jesus wanted people to stop feeling *sufficiently* righteous, *sufficiently* virtuous, *sufficiently* good. He wanted people to aim higher. He urged people to turn from life-draining lower impulses and be motivated by higher impulses: love, compassion, generosity, hope. He exhorted his listeners to leave behind the dead world of *complacency* and ascend to the vibrant world of continual spiritual growth.

So Jesus' ideas are consistent with the view that resurrection is a *process* that starts in this mortal realm and carries over into the immortal realm. Thus death is not a state, but a *transition*. And we are not passive with respect to resurrection, but *active*.

If resurrection begins now, then it's unlikely that any good thought or deed will get discarded or left behind when we experience death. Everything that is worthwhile will be connected to bigger, longer-lasting picture. Author and former pastor Rob Bell offers his opinion on the matter:

> "Jesus invites us to trust resurrection, that every glimmer of good, every hint of hope, every impulse that elevates the soul, is a sign, a taste, a glimpse of how things actually are, and how things ultimately will be."[42]

Conclusion

Something happened to motivate a group of despondent, deflated individuals to start spreading the faith of Jesus with enthusiasm and fearlessness. That is undeniable. They interpreted what they had experienced using the idea of resurrection, which for them meant rising from death. (And although they saw resurrection as an *event*, it was significant only within the context of Jesus' *life*.)

But we don't have to be perpetually bound to the ancient way of looking at resurrection. We can apply a fresh and contemporary perspective to the idea without diminishing its power. Resurrection doesn't have to mean a *return* to life from the state of death. It can mean the ongoing process of spiritual growth that begins now and continues, uninterrupted by death, into the immortal realm. And I think this is something that Jesus was getting at in his teachings.

Jesus seemed to expand the idea of resurrection to include everyday life. He wanted people to leave behind the dead path that "leads to destruction," and to lift themselves up to the vibrant path that "leads to life."[43] He stressed the value of continually striving to rise above destructive thoughts and habits so we could live abundantly. He seemed to think that we could begin the resurrection process *here and now*, actively taking steps to ascend to a higher quality of life that death cannot degrade.

Summary

Five years ago I understood resurrection only from the traditional perspective. I thought that the matter had been settled, and that no analysis or scrutiny was necessary or worthwhile. But as I learned more about resurrection, and set aside my preconceptions, I eventually gained a more reasonable understanding of the idea and its true significance in my life.

Update to what I know

I now know that there is no doubt that Jesus experienced resurrection. His followers were dejected and without hope, but soon something dramatic happened to energize them. Resurrection happened. They realized that their Master was still very much with them. And the

Christian faith began in that certain awareness of Jesus' continued existence.

The pertinent question is: How can I best interpret resurrection today? The ancient view, held by the followers of Jesus, involved a body "rising from death" (with some debate about what "body" actually meant). But I don't have to be bound to this way of interpreting resurrection. I can believe in eternal life without clinging to an interpretation that today might not be the most useful one. Immortality doesn't have to be understood within its original framework to be a meaningful and vital idea.

After looking at what Jesus taught, I believe that he tried to recast resurrection as an experience that begins here and now. It was not just about "death then life"; it was about "life then death then life." He changed the focus and stressed the *ongoing* process of resurrection, of rebirth. He urged people to lift themselves up continually to a better quality of life—a life in God's kingdom.

Course change

Based on what I've learned, I have decided to give up the traditional church view of resurrection and instead to follow Jesus. Although he accepted the idea that resurrection made death insignificant, he also seemed to understand that resurrection can be part of everyday life. He challenged people to rise above the lifeless world of sinfulness and complacency and ascend to the level of abundant living. He wanted everyone to follow the challenging path that makes that kind of existence possible.

I think Jesus added a much-needed practical dimension to the concept of resurrection. And I think I can benefit more from embracing his ideas about being actively involved in resurrection than I can from adhering to a formal church doctrine.

So the traditional view—that resurrection began with a one-time miraculous event—is no longer workable. My Christian faith no longer depends on resurrection being a particular type of *event*. It depends on Jesus being a particular type of *individual:* someone who understood that resurrection begins in this world, and continues without interruption through death and beyond as we continually ascend to more meaningful levels of existence. Thus resurrection is no longer a historical event that I merely acknowledge. Instead, it is a dynamic process in which I can *participate*. What an exciting and liberating perspective!

Notes

[1] Shakespeare, William. "Hamlet," Act 3, Scene 1, http://shakespeare.mit.edu/hamlet/hamlet.3.1.html

[2] "Resurrection." *Encyclopaedia Britannica*, https://www.britannica.com/topic/resurrection-religion

[3] Smith, Lani. "Jubilation!" Dayton, Ohio: Lorenz Publishing Company, 1971.

[4] Borg, Marcus. "A Chronological New Testament." HuffPost, 2012, https://www.huffpost.com/entry/a-chronological-new-testament_b_1823018

[5] 1 Corinthians 15:3-8

[6] 1 Corinthians 15:52-53

[7] Fosdick, Harry Emerson. *A Guide to Understanding the Bible*. New York: Harper & Row, Publishers, 1938.

[8] Tabor, James. "The 'Strange' Ending of the Gospel of Mark and Why It Makes All the Difference." Biblical Archeology Society, 2018, https://www.biblicalarchaeology.org/daily/biblical-topics/new-testament/the-strange-ending-of-the-gospel-of-mark-and-why-it-makes-all-the-difference/

[9] Mark 16:6

[10] "Compare Biblical Accounts of the Resurrection." ReligionFacts.com, 2017, http://www.religionfacts.com/charts/resurrection-accounts

[11] Ehrman, Bart. "If Jesus Never Called Himself God, How Did He Become One?" Transcript of "Fresh Air" radio broadcast. National Public Radio, 2014, https://www.npr.org/2014/04/07/300246095/if-jesus-never-called-himself-god-how-did-he-become-one

[12] John 20:26-27

[13] Luke 9:22

[14] Fosdick, Harry Emerson. *A Guide to Understanding the Bible*. New York: Harper & Row, Publishers, 1938.

[15] Achtemeier, Paul J., ed. "Resurrection." *The HarperCollins Bible Dictionary*. San Francisco: HarperOne, 1996.

[16] Isaiah 26:19

[17] Mark 12:18-27

[18] Fosdick, Harry Emerson. *A Guide to Understanding the Bible*. New York, Harper & Row, Publishers, 1938.

[19] 1 Corinthians 15:20, 22

[20] Romans 6:4

[21] Achtemeier, Paul J., ed. "Resurrection." *The HarperCollins Bible Dictionary*. San Francisco: HarperOne, 1996.

[22] Luke 29:37-38

[23] John 5:28-29

[24] John 6:40

[25] Spong, John Shelby. "Gospel of John: What Everyone Should Know About The Fourth Gospel." HuffPost, 2013, https://www.huffpost.com/entry/gospel-of-john-what-everyone-knows-about-the-fourth-gospel_b_3422026

[26] Tuckett, Christopher. *Christology and the New Testament*, chapter 9: "The Gospel of John," pp.151-152.

[27] Matthew 18:20

[28] Luke 24:50-51

[29] 1 Corinthians 15:22-23

[30] 1 Thessalonians 4:16-17

[31] "Resurrection." *Internet Encyclopedia of Philosophy.* Fieser, James, and Dowden, Bradley, eds., https://www.iep.utm.edu/resurrec/

[32] Mark 13:24-27

[33] Mounce, William. "Lecture 7: Mark 13." BiblicalTraining, https://www.biblicaltraining.org/library/mark-13/new-testament/william-mounce

[34] Matthew 16:28

[35] 1 Corinthians 15:3-8

[36] Adams, James Rowe. "What Can Progressive Christians Say About Resurrection?" Progressive Christianity, 2006, https://progressivechristianity.org/resources/what-can-progressive-christians-say-about-resurrection/

[37] Lowry, Robert. "Low in the Grave He Lay." *Baptist Hymnal.* Nashville, Tennessee: Convention Press, 1956.

[38] Korb, Scott. Quoted in Winston, Kimberley. "Gospel story of Jesus' resurrection a source of deep rifts in Christian religion." *The Washington Post,* 2014, https://www.washingtonpost.com/local/gospel-story-of-jesus-resurrection-a-source-of-deep-rifts-in-christian-religion/2014/04/18/7c715c0a-c6fa-11e3-8b9a-8e0977a24aeb_story.html

[39] Matthew 18:22

[40] Matthew 18:3

[41] Matthew 21:21

[42] Bell, Rob. "Resurrection" video. 2010, https://www.youtube.com/watch?v=3s5gq9BmGDU

[43] Matthew 7:13-14

6. Assessment

Over the past few years, as I tried to examine Jesus without relying on assumptions or preconceptions, I found a surprising perspective—one that in many ways does not align with the traditional church perspective. The carved-in-stone doctrines and dogmas and creeds that have become so important are not evident in Jesus' unique way of looking at the world. They may be comforting and familiar, and "essential" according to some, but they in fact obscure Jesus' actual views on the fundamental elements of faith. And once we remove the theological structures that have been erected over the centuries, Jesus' radical and enlightened way of seeing things emerges. I call it the Jesus Perspective.

In this chapter I want to summarize what I've learned from my research and explain how it is relevant to anyone, Christian or not, who wants to think more critically and intelligently about faith. When we confront *authentic* Christianity, without the unnecessary complications added along the way, we find a view of life that is uniquely empowering, uplifting, and irresistible.

The Jesus Perspective

As I see it, the Jesus Perspective has four primary characteristics:

1) It is practical

Jesus didn't spend a lot of time talking about abstract concepts. He talked about ideas and actions that were useful in everyday life. He gave people strategies for dealing with the common problems that interfere with abundant living. Notice the practical nature of his teachings:

- Jesus rejected the view that every element of the law had value, even though that was widely accepted, and stressed that any law that was not useful should be abandoned. Avoid helping people on the Sabbath because religious leaders say so? No, said Jesus, place human needs above the minutiae of the law.[1] He wanted us to be saved from *static faith*, which stresses slavish adherence to traditional views, and replace it with *dynamic faith*, which allows us to intelligently adapt principles so they at all times can help us to live fully.

- Jesus devalued the tendency to elevate ourselves above others, which is nearly universal, and encouraged us to strive for accurate perception of ourselves and our neighbors. Draw attention to your neighbor's flaws? No, said Jesus, come to grips with your own flaws that prevent you from reaching your full human potential.[2] He wanted us to be saved from *egotism*, which leads to unproductive criticism and judgment, and replace it with *humility*, which leads to tolerance and realistic expectations, thereby making meaningful relationships possible.

• Jesus disapproved of ostentatious displays of piety and virtue, despite their popularity, and insisted that they do not improve the quality of life. Pray loudly so people can be impressed with your righteousness? No, said Jesus, go into your room and pray privately so you can connect with God on a personal and meaningful level.[3] He wanted us to be saved from valuing *outward change*, which emphasizes appearance more than substance, and replace it with valuing *inward change*, which reflects authentic spiritual growth and maturity.

2) It is affirmative

Jesus didn't focus on the negative. He didn't spend his time berating people and focusing on their faults. Instead, he tried to see people in a positive light. He looked past the outward imperfections and imagined the child of God within each individual. Take a look at the affirmative nature of his ideas:

• Jesus discarded the notion that we enter this world fallen and broken, even though it was a popular view, and encouraged people to understand their innate wholeness. Approach God as a self-proclaimed miserable sinner? No, said Jesus, approach God as a little child so we can enter His kingdom in our original blessed condition.[4] He wanted people to be saved from *self loathing*, built on the idea that we are basically bad, and replace it with *healthy self esteem*, built on the idea that we all are, from birth, members of a divine family.

• Jesus rebutted the idea that God is angry, capricious, and demanding, despite the fact that most saw Him that way, and offered his belief in a helpful and friendly God. Try your best, with rituals and pious observances, to avoid God's wrath? No, said

Jesus, try your best, with prayer and repentance, to approach God's love.[5] He wanted us to be saved from *fear of God the despot*, who wants to punish us, and replace it with *pursuit of God the Father*, who wants to love and guide us.

• Jesus repudiated the gloomy concept that the universe is impersonal and unaccommodating, even though that view was widely held, and taught that the opposite is the reality. Struggle just to get by in a life that goes nowhere? No, said Jesus, "knock and the door will be opened"; in other words, realize limitless possibilities by *acting as if* all things are possible.[6] He wanted us to be saved from *cynicism* about life, and replace it with boundless *optimism* and the understanding that God has given us all we need to survive and thrive.

3) It is transformative

Jesus didn't encourage people to follow rules and regulations without question. He knew that such mindless obedience would not produce the real change of heart needed for them to gain entry into God's kingdom. Instead he focused on real inward change that comes when we fully grasp our place in God's family. Consider the transformative nature of his beliefs:

• Jesus scrapped the idea that we can become sufficiently righteous, despite the fact that most people believed that, and encouraged people to go beyond what they thought to be adequate. Forgive people as many as seven times? No, said Jesus, forgive so many times that you lose count.[7] He wanted us to be saved from *complacency*, based on the belief that we have arrived, and replace it with the *drive to grow*, which helps us to focus on the journey and the possibility of rising continually to new levels of spiritual competence.

• Jesus threw out the notion that worldly values are grounded in reality, which was a commonly held belief, and said that they are in fact out of alignment with reality. Implement the "eye for an eye" strategy when someone offends you? No, said Jesus, love and pray for those who offend you.[8] He wanted us to be saved from *conventional values*, which are earth-bound and limited, and replace them with counter-intuitive *kingdom values*, which transcend time and place.

• Jesus abandoned the idea that the goal of living is ease and comfort, which most people aspired to, and urged people to take a more vigorous approach to life. Follow the easy path and just get by? No, said Jesus, take up our crosses—in other words, keep challenging ourselves, aiming higher, and dreaming bigger.[9] He wanted us to be saved from *satisfaction*, which leads to adequate living, and replace it with *creative discontent*, which motivates us to go beyond mere existence.

4) It is hopeful

Jesus didn't see people as helpless or hopeless. He saw in people limitless possibilities for growth and improvement. And behind it all was the idea that the universe is purposeful, that it has a divine order. And we can align ourselves with it if we choose. Notice the hopeful nature of Jesus' message:

• Jesus discredited the idea that reconciliation with God is a complicated process, which was a popular view, and put forth a different view. Seek atonement with sacrifices, rituals, asceticism, and long-winded prayers? No, said Jesus, confess and repent, and choose to turn away from destructive thoughts, feelings, and actions.[10] He wanted us to be saved from *weak resolve*, which can lead to frustration, guilt, and shame when we make mistakes, and replace it with *steadfastness* as we try to stay the course and fully grasp our innate oneness with God.

• Jesus jettisoned the concept that we are by nature evil, despite the popularity of that view, and emphasized our natural goodness. Accept the dismal idea that we are merely two-legged animals, following instincts? No, said Jesus, realize that we are the light of the world, made in God's image.[11] He wanted us to be saved from the immature tendency to be motivated by *base impulses*, which choke off the life force, and replace it with the commitment to be motivated by *higher impulses*—love, compassion, mercy, helpfulness.

• Jesus set aside the idea that God is "out there," which was the conventional view, and exhorted people to understand that God is close by and always available. Hope to be rewarded with access to God's kingdom off in the future? No, said Jesus, choose to enter the kingdom here and now.[12] He wanted us to be saved from the idea that heaven is a *place* far away, and replace it with the idea that heaven is a *dynamic state of being* that is accessible through faith in our everyday lives.

Summary

When we adopt the Jesus Perspective, we are saved from a bland existence. No more unremarkable dreams, no more mediocre generosity, no more so-so morality. The Jesus Perspective shines a bright light on our limitless capacity to live fully, love unconditionally, and grow spiritually. And it happens on the path that Jesus blazed, one day at a time, one step at a time. By gradually letting go of conventional values and following Jesus, we begin to accept abundant living as our birthright.

Jesus continually raised the bar when it came to righteousness. He didn't expect people to reach the bar—but he knew that everyone could *try* to reach the bar. And it is in the trying that growth takes place. When we strive to improve, we naturally leave behind the erroneous idea that we have achieved perfection. So Jesus emphasized the value of growing, improving, and ascending as we live by faith. His focus was on the *process* of living, on the journey, on the dynamic nature of our life-long development as children of a loving heavenly Father.

I believe that the whole point of the Jesus Perspective is to challenge us to see things not in terms of earthly values, but in terms of kingdom values. Jesus wanted to shake us out of our comfort zone. He wanted us to question conventional wisdom and think critically and deeply about the fundamental elements of faith. He wanted us to see things in a new way that gives us the power, resolve, and courage needed to maximize our God-given human potential. Amen!

Notes

[1] Matthew 12:11-12
[2] Matthew 7:3-5
[3] Matthew 6:5-6

[4] Matthew 18:3
[5] Luke 5:32, Luke 15:7
[6] Mark 11:24
[7] Matthew 18:22
[8] Matthew 5:44
[9] Matthew 16:24-26
[10] Luke 13:5
[11] Matthew 16:24-26
[12] Matthew 4:17

7. Path Christianity

The four obvious characteristics of the Jesus Perspective—
practical, affirmative, transformative, hopeful—give us a
name for Jesus' unique type of faith: Path Christianity. And
this name makes sense because of Jesus' emphasis on the
freedom we have to choose our path:

> "Enter through the narrow gate; for the gate is
> wide and the road is easy that leads to destruc-
> tion, and there are many who take it. For the
> gate is narrow and the road is hard that leads to
> life, and there are few who find it."[1]

Clearly, Jesus understood that life is a journey, and that
the elements of faith must be *worked out* as we go about the
business of living.

As I see it, the Jesus Perspective creates a path *of* salvation
(not a path *to* salvation). Thus salvation is something we *discover* on the path. It's a dynamic, gradual awareness and
acceptance of God's unconditional love, generosity, and grace,
and of our commitment to living abundantly.

But we're not saved from some hellish punishment imagined by people in ancient times. We're saved in a very practical way from those things that inhibit abundant living: fear, shame, guilt, anger, hatred. These are all things that we can remove from our path when we adopt the Jesus Perspective. So salvation is not something supernatural off in the future, but a practical experience that can take place *over time* as we gradually align ourselves with divine purpose.

Path Christianity is based on the unembellished life and faith of Jesus, someone who embraced his innate divinity in a way that startled, confounded, and inspired. And he wanted others to have the spiritual life that he had, to live fearlessly and confidently as he did.

Over time Jesus demonstrated that he had become *optimally receptive* to God's love, grace, and power. We know this because of the reactions of those who knew him best: his disciples. They saw in him an unsurpassed spiritual quality. They marveled at the intensity of his faith. And they believed that he demonstrated what divinity looks like in everyday life.

Jesus shared his perspective that allowed the divine to be revealed in him. He knew that we could do the same if we were properly informed and motivated. After all, he said, "follow me."[2] He wanted everyone to think as he thought and live as he lived.

Path Christianity is:

> *Practical*, focusing only on what contributes to the development of healthy mind, body, and spirit in everyday life.

> *Affirmative*, accentuating only what is positive, uplifting, and helpful in maximizing our God-given potential.

> *Transformative*, stressing only what helps to bring about the true inward change needed to allow God to reveal Himself in us.

> *Hopeful*, emphasizing only what creates
> boundless optimism that makes it possible to
> overcome problems and live abundantly.

Path Christianity gives little weight to dogmas, doctrines, creeds, and rituals that were created long after Jesus put forth his views. Instead it seeks to eliminate the elaborate theological structures that have been imposed on Jesus, and return to his unique method for getting the most from life.

Path Christianity views the traditional elements of the faith—among them incarnation and atonement—not as *events* that we merely observe and believe, but as *processes* in which we participate. Thus it places importance on responsibility, involvement, and continual progress. This is the challenging path that Jesus said "leads to life."[3]

So Path Christianity places emphasis not on the destination, but on the *journey*. It focuses on simple (but often counterintuitive) steps, put forth by Jesus, that we can take to make ourselves optimally receptive to God's love, grace, and power. As we do so, we come to fully grasp the reality that we are part of God's family—loved, trusted, and empowered. When we learn to embrace that conception, we naturally start to remove the impediments to abundant living. We naturally start to be saved in a very practical way from those emotions, thoughts, and actions that restrict the flow of life.

In Path Christianity, the cross reminds us that there are two paths that we can follow in life. The intuitive path ($-$) restricts us to the earthy realm; the path of Jesus (|) connects us with the divine realm. One path is uncreative; the other creative. One path binds us; the other frees us. One path is mundane; the other exciting. The phrase "Jesus crossed my path" captures the essence of this fundamental idea.

Embracing Path Christianity helps us to realize our potential, remove barriers to healthy living, and align ourselves with divine purpose. It helps us to be of the "same mind"[4] as Jesus regarding oneness with God. And when we adopt the

Jesus Perspective, everything changes. As we become aware of God's very real presence, the process of continual rebirth begins. Then we start to see limitless possibilities.

Imagine what would happen if this new (2000 year old) type of faith, free of pointless theological complications, started to spread!

Notes

[1] Matthew 7:13-14
[2] Matthew 4:19
[3] Matthew 7:13-14
[4] Philippians 2:5

One more thing

I hope you've found *The Jesus Perspective* to be helpful and thought provoking. If so, please post an online review so the book can gain momentum and spread this vigorous interpretation of the Good News to a wider audience. And if you have comments or questions about the book, you can contact me via my website, artspace5.com.

Robert Harris